Not Your Mother's Book . . .
On Cats

Created and Edited by
Dahlynn McKowen,
Ken McKowen and Margie Yee Webb

Published by
Publishing Syndicate LLC

PO Box 607
Orangevale California 95662
www.PublishingSyndicate.com

Not Your Mother's Book . . .
On Cats

*We would like to thank the many individuals
who granted us permission to reprint their stories.
See the complete listing beginning on page 286.*

Edited by Dahlynn McKowen,
Ken McKowen and Margie Yee Webb
Cover and Book Design by Publishing Syndicate
Cover photo: Sarah Fields Photography/Shutterstock.com
Copyeditor: Dahlynn McKowen
Proofreader: Pat Nelson

Published by
Publishing Syndicate LLC
PO Box 607
Orangevale California 95662

www.PublishingSyndicate.com
www.Facebook.com/PublishingSyndicate
Twitter: @PublishingSynd

Print Edition ISBN: 978-1-938778-18-6
EPUB Digital Edition ISBN: 978-1-938778-19-3
MOBI Digital Edition ISBN 978-938778-31-5
Library of Congress Control Number 2013907708

Printed in Canada.

This book is a collaborative effort. Writers from all over the world submitted their work for consideration, with 62 stories making the final cut. All contributors are compensated for their stories.

Publishing Syndicate strongly encourages you to submit your story for one of its many upcoming anthologies.

For information on how to submit your story, go to www.PublishingSyndicate.com.

Dedication

This book is dedicated to my loving Cat Mulan who let me stalk her with my camera to capture her expressive personality and who sparked my creativity and inspired me to pursue writing.

I also dedicate this book to the Front Street Animal Shelter in Sacramento, California, Cat Mulan's sanctuary before she adopted me in 2004. Their amazing work has helped many animals to find forever homes.

And last, this book is dedicated to all the devoted people who make a difference in the lives of cats and other companion animals—thank you!

~~ Margie Yee Webb

Cat Mulan

CONTENTS

4 The Games Felines Play

5 The Joy of Cats

6 Pussies Galore!

7 Cat-astrophe!

8 The Stray-Cat Strut

Acknowledgments

You all are the cat's meow!

From Margie

Thank you to my cat—Cat Mulan. You bring me joy, smiles and laughter.

Thank you to my friends, especially at the California Writers Club and the Cat Writers' Association. I enjoyed reading the submissions about your precious cats.

And last, thank you to my family for your love and support in my writing endeavors.

From Dahlynn and Ken

Thank you to Dahlynn's teen son Shawn. Another book is done, and now that you finally have your own car, you don't have to stick around for all the craziness of the next book!

Thank you to our 11-year-old dog Shilo. She kept us company during days and days of editing CAT stories, and she helped look through all the wonderful CAT photos submitted for consideration. Shilo was on the brink of crazy every time Dahlynn—aka, Mom—said the word "CAT!" aloud, as one of Shilo's jobs is to keep cats away from her 10 beloved exotic chickens. Now you can relax, Old Girl.

And thank you to Pat Nelson for proofing yet another book. Your expertise and, more importantly, your friendship and support mean the world to us.

And from all of us at Publishing Syndicate

A special thanks to the many writers who submitted stories for this book. Without you, this book would not have come together like it did. Your stories are wonderful and we thank you for sharing them with us and the world. We only wish we could have printed every story submitted.

Keep those stories coming in for future NYMB titles: www.PublishingSyndicate.com.

Introduction

"Cats rule the world."
~~ Jim Davis, creator of the
comic strip Garfield

Jim Davis' comic strip *Garfield* is one of my favorites. I've learned that no two cats are alike. They may be the same breed or similar in physical appearance, but each has its own personality, its own way of thinking, its own likes and dislikes. For example, my cat doesn't eat lasagna or drink coffee—two of Garfield's favorite foods. She also doesn't have a dog for a sidekick or a stuffed teddy bear named "Pooky." Instead, my cat is adventurous, free-spirited and curious. But she does like to sleep, which is something she has in common with the Big Orange Cat.

I have also learned that one can never second-guess a cat. Cats rule the world and have their humans trained. We spoil them, we love them. We cater to their every whim and rejoice in their every accomplishment. There are times when our feline friends make us upset, such as when they bring uninvited guests—like lizards, snakes or mice—into our homes. But that is to be expected, because cats do the unexpected. As Garfield says, "Never trust a smiling cat."

Recently, I happened upon the word "ailurophile." It means, "A cat fancier or lover of cats." That's me, and that's you. And that's what you'll find in this book: first-person stories written mostly by ailurophiles and a few non-ailurophiles, the latter sharing stories about their cat-loving friends and family. There is always a cat story to be told and many laughs to be had.

I close with a quote that Garfield would absolutely agree with—a quote from his namesake, President James A. Garfield: "Man cannot live by bread alone; he must have peanut butter." And a good book—this book. Enjoy!

~~ Margie Yee Webb

Love and Hisses

Affection all around!

Can You See Me?

by
Dena Harris

When she was little, my sister used to poke her fingers beneath the bathroom door and wiggle them.

"Can you see me?" she'd ask.

"Go away," whoever was inside would answer.

She would shove her hand further beneath the door.

"Now? Can you see me now?"

"Yes, I see you now. Can you go away for a few minutes?"

The hand would disappear and there would be a light thud as she leaned her small body against the door.

"When are you coming out?"

We were all happy to see that phase end, and I thought my days of being stalked through closed doors were over. I admit to giggling when friends moaned about how their children never left them alone, even when they were in the bathroom.

"Should've had cats," I informed them smugly.

But my life of bathroom solitude has been upended. Both cats have recently decided they can't abide a closed door, be it a closet door, bedroom door, or—you guessed it—bathroom door.

They scared the daylights out of me the first time. I awoke in the middle of the night and felt my way to the bathroom. Half asleep, I had just closed the door when suddenly, *whump*! The bathroom door flew open, and a small tabby cat stood illuminated in the doorway. She gazed steadily at me before turning away. My heart raced. I felt like I'd been given a warning visit by the Kitty Mafia. Keep the door open—or else.

The next morning, I alerted my husband. "Better lock the door when you're in the bathroom."

"Why?"

"It's the cats," I said, looking over my shoulder. "They don't like closed doors."

"Uh-huh," he said slowly. "And I should be concerned . . . why?"

But Mister Oh-So-Smart wasn't laughing when the cats body-slammed the bathroom door open while he was inside. I was upstairs when I heard his call for help.

"Would you get the cats out of here?" he asked. "I'd like some privacy."

So we started locking the door. That's when tiny paws began to appear underneath the closed door. It was cute for a while. A tiny white paw would slide beneath the door and tap the floor.

But then there was the talking. Finding the door wouldn't budge and unable to reach us from beneath the door, the cats would sit outside the locked door and "talk" to the person inside.

"Mrow. Rowr-rowr. Mow?" (When are you coming out?)

The best though, was coming home early and finding both cats sitting outside the bathroom where my husband had locked himself in. He was talking back to them.

"Rowr? Meow, meow," said the cats.

"Yeah, I know. I hate when that happens," he answered through the closed door.

"Purr, rowr-meow."

"Really? So what did you say back?"

"Mow! Psfft! Meow."

"Ah, ha ha," he said. "You are so clever."

"Honey?" I knocked. "Everything OK?"

There was a moment of silence. "I have no idea what you're talking about," he called back.

I wasn't letting him off that easy. I squatted on the floor and wriggled my fingers beneath the door. "Can you see me?" I asked.

"Go away," he said.

I scratched on the door. "So when are you coming out?"

"The minute I do I'm having you committed," he warned. "Go away!"

And so it went. We had pretty much resigned ourselves to the situation when luck struck. I went into the bathroom one day without bothering to close the door. No cats appeared.

Excellent, I thought. I shared my discovery that night with my husband.

"I broke the code!" I said. "We need to adopt an open-door policy. If you don't close the door, they take no interest in what you're doing."

He seemed less than thrilled. "But I like closing the door."

I sighed. "Close the door and have an audience or enjoy the peace of an open one. It's your choice."

"I miss our life before cats," he said.

He had a point. It was nice when we had some say over the ajar status of doors in our home. Still, even with all the bother, it's nice knowing you are so important to someone that every minute apart counts.

"Mrow?"

Yes, I'll be out soon.

Big Game

by
Dr. Stephanie Burk

When September arrives in southwest Ohio, sportsmen everywhere gear up for hunting season.

I'm not particularly excited about this annual sport, but once upon a time, I went on my own September hunt. My quarry? A small yellow cat.

I was standing at a Quickie Mart gas pump when I heard the sound feared by all who already own too many cats—a yowl of distress. That's when I spied a blond kitten just across the busy state highway.

Knowing I had to do something, I decided to rescue it, with the hopes that some kindly client at my small animal veterinary practice would willingly adopt such an engaging baby. Rescuing a kitten seemed simple enough, but whenever I got close to this minuscule specimen, it disappeared into the bushes like a puff of sulfur smoke. I finally gave up, planning to resume the hunt after work. But I resigned my-self to the fact that I may find nothing left of it but a banana-colored smear on the road.

When I returned later, the kitten was still howling vigor-ously from the underbrush. After an hour, I remained emp-ty-handed. Again, I left reluctantly, promising it I'd be back. I was troubled, but determined. The kitten didn't care.

This dance of ours went on for several days. I grew in-creasingly glassy-eyed and desperate, losing sleep over what had ballooned into a full-scale obsession. The kitten was des-tined to become a saffron pancake if I didn't succeed, and soon. It did seem to know its way through the thicket of weeds and scrubby trees, as did I, a result of my rescue at-tempts.

A change of strategy was clearly in order. And as luck would have it, a new plan presented itself in the middle of my restless night. I sat up in bed, dislodging several slumber-ing dogs. *You are a VET. You can drug him into a stupor!* I told myself. *Brilliant.*

Armed with canned food, cat sedative and my game bag—a pillowcase hanging like a flag from the waistband of my jeans—I sought my prey. It was there, yowling away at me. I sallied once more into the thicket and the fray.

The kitten readily wolfed down his drugged cat food. I waved away mosquitoes that had joined the party, and I waited. The kitten became a little uncoordinated, but no slower. More food, more sedatives—I gave it enough to fell a belligerent Rottweiler. No luck. It ate more, it slept not at all.

Rats. I can't quit! I knew that if the kitten decided—in a drug-induced haze—to stagger onto the road, its demise would be entirely my fault.

So I persevered. Two hot, humid hours later, the kitten was mellow, but still elusive, and I was at the end of my rope. I decided on a new tactic—I would hunt the little bastard down like a Redbone hound after a 20-pound raccoon.

I pushed deeper into the brush, enthusiastically escorted by the growing swarm of mosquitoes. I herded the kitten away from the road and it shot up a ruined tree trunk.

This particular tree looked like something from a fantasy movie set. Lightening had split it into three parts. Two pieces of trunk still pointed upright like horns, while the majority of the tree—minus its top—had broken off and was resting at a 45-degree angle. The kitten was perched about 10 feet over my head, looking worried.

The tension and the mosquito cloud thickened rapidly. I slithered up the rotting stump, some 3 feet off the ground, and stretched tentatively along the length of the trunk, hoping it would hold. My quarry remained out of reach. I tried cautiously shaking the trunk and rattling nearby branches. No luck, with the exception that the tree didn't fall over with me on it.

I wheedled, cajoled, chatted with God, swore and even fed the mosquitoes while I was perched precariously on that tree. Finally, I broke off a branch of a bush within my grasp and rustled it above the kitten. It looked panicky. I rustled harder. It squinted down at me, sizing up the situation, possibly considering leaping over my head. It inched closer and hunkered down, gathering itself for that leap of faith.

What happened next? I'm not certain. There was a wild scramble and a drop of several feet. Somehow, I managed to nab the kitten in midair and wrestle it to the ground.

"Scream all you want!" I panted to the terrified kitten, clutching the scruff of its neck. "I'm not letting go!"

My sanity depended on keeping a tight grip on my quarry. I whipped the flannel game bag from the back of my pants and swaddled the kitten in it, but not before it managed to sink two tiny teeth into my thumb.

I staggered from the thicket, pulling twigs out of my hair, wiping sweat from my eyes and triumphantly clutching the fussing, furious pillowcase. Disheveled but victorious, I had become a successful hunter.

And where is my trophy now? Sprawled out on the table next to me. His name is Toby.

You didn't honestly think I'd give him away after all that effort, did you?

Toby helping wrap Christmas presents

Grandpa and Juliet

by

Barbara Carpenter

My husband has never been a fan of indoor pets—cats or dogs. "I don't want dog or cat hair all over the furniture!" was his motto.

When two of our grandchildren brought a couple of half-grown house cats to live on our farm one winter day, Grandpa declared that Juliet and Rascal would become barn felines. The children weren't happy about that. The mother of the kittens, who was named Fireball, maintained her lofty position as queen at my daughter's house.

Grandpa arranged a warm bed for the cats. He placed a heavy base of straw, covered amply with discarded woolen afghans, in a wooden box, well away from any drafts. That evening, he made a few extra trips outdoors, ostensibly to check the weather. But, I knew he was checking on the cats.

The next morning, he returned home only minutes after leaving for work.

"What did you forget?" I asked.

"We've had an accident," he said. "One of the cats was under the hood when I started the truck."

"Oh, no!" I cried. "Which one?"

"Jessica's," he said. Eleven-year-old Jessica had named the beautiful, longhaired, black-and-white kitten "Juliet." Why? Because she looked like a Juliet. Thirteen-year-old Nick had named his male kitten "Rascal"—for obvious reasons—although the yellow tabby was gentle enough.

"Is she dead?" I asked. My husband shook his head.

"No, but her leg is broken."

"Well, gather her up and we'll take her to the vet," I told him.

He grumbled all the way to the barn. "Stupid cat is going to cost me a hundred bucks."

"It doesn't matter," I called after him. "It's Jessica's cat, and you've got to take care of her!"

I held the poor kitty on the way to the doctor. Sweet natured, she lay in my arms as if she knew we were going to help her.

"Oh, it's not too bad," our local veterinarian told us upon examining Juliet. "It's a clean break, so we'll just put her to sleep and set it."

"While she's asleep, can you spay her?" I asked.

"Yes, we can," he replied. "It's a perfect time to do it, since she's going to be laid up for a while." My husband raised his eyebrows and opened his mouth. I narrowed my eyes and returned his stare. He looked away. The vet said we could pick her up the next afternoon.

On the way back to the truck, my husband said, "That stupid cat is going to cost me $500!" I just looked at him, and he didn't say another word.

Shortly after we arrived home, I got a call from the doctor. "Mrs. Carpenter, we have a problem," he said. My heart sank. My first thought was that Juliet had died, followed by the thought that she was probably pregnant. "It seems that Juliet is . . ." he paused for effect ". . . a boy!"

After a long moment, I laughed aloud. "So underneath all that beautiful hair is a male?" It was just too wonderful a tale . . . no homonym-al pun intended.

"Do you want me to perform the same procedure on him?" the doctor asked.

"Absolutely! What's good for Juliet is good for Romeo!" I laughed. He chuckled, too.

"I suppose you could call him 'Jules,' instead of Juliet," the vet suggested.

I told my husband about the mistaken identity of Juliet, and that I had asked the doctor to neuter him. "Why did you do that? He wouldn't have kittens!" He visibly cringed at the thought! I think he was suffering from pain transference in sympathy, one male for another.

"No, but he would have sprinkled them liberally throughout the neighborhood. It will keep him at home," I said. "Besides, what's fair for a her is fair for a him!"

On the way to pick up the injured kitty, we bought a litter box, Kitty Litter, a feeding bowl and anything we could think of to make Juliet/Jules comfortable through his recovery. Already house broken, he was easy to care for. And even my husband was sympathetic and gentle with him.

My story would have ended right there, but for one circumstance. Two days later, my elderly stepfather passed away, and as such, my siblings and I had to join our mother in Arizona, some 1,800 miles from our home in Illinois. My husband, the militant anti-housecat advocate, had responsibility for the total care and feeding of the injured cat. Not only did he care for him, he cleaned the litter box and fed and watered him. By the time I returned home six days later, the cat had discovered a comfortable after-dinner position— upon my husband's lap.

In April, quite some time after Juliet's leg had healed, my husband stated that it was still too cold for the poor little thing to stay outdoors with his brother, Rascal, who had become a splendid barn cat. Eventually, Juliet did join Rascal outdoors. He loved it, and he waved his plume of a tail high in the air as he pranced across the lawn. All he had to do was meow at the door, and Grandpa let him in. Juliet-in-drag, for as long as he lived, retained his special place in the heart of my husband, the rugged, hard-edged marshmallow.

Juliet with a camera-shy Grandpa

Breakfast with the Queen

by
Sheree K. Nielsen

As the toaster sprang forth my perfectly tanned pumpernickel bread, I sensed a fat, black presence in my peripheral vision. It was Midnight, our cat.

More than eight years have passed since my husband rescued Midnight on a snowy evening in November. She lay trembling in a pool of motor oil under our car outside his favorite coffee shop. Dull and sticky, her fur was atrocious. There was no telling how long she'd been hiding under cars.

Hubby scooped up the filthy feline in his arms, placed her in his big blue Buick and headed to our vet's office, located across the street from the coffeehouse. The microchip beneath her skin revealed that the owner had left no forwarding address and no phone number. *A possible prank? A black cat purchased for Halloween, shunned after that scary night?*

With intentions of only fostering, we welcomed the kitty into our home until she could be placed with a suitable family. I wasn't particularly fond of female cats. Firsthand experiences recounted by friends and neighbors reinforced my fear of their bad temperament and tendency to destroy furniture.

A degreasing, recommended by our vet, was in order for our houseguest. Midnight and my hubby bonded as he washed away her troubles and past lives with dishwashing liquid. Confined to solitary to clear up fleas and worms, she spent 10 days in the master bathroom. While doing her time gracefully, Midnight chatted to birds and squirrels from the picture windows. Inquisitively, she watched as I applied my morning makeup. Hubby always conversed with her while showering and that seemed to make her happy.

As soon as Midnight was released from confinement, we introduced her to the rest of the animal family. (Scooby and Tripoli, our male cats, sat patiently on the other side of the bathroom door for more than a week, anticipating her arrival.)

It took a couple of months, but with her persuasive personality, she managed to easily dominate the cats and two female dogs. And us. The street kitty blossomed into royalty, and we all found ourselves under her spell. "Her Serene Highness" soon became a permanent family member.

Most mornings, whenever I lifted the black ceramic cover off the butter dish, Midnight invaded my personal space. She loved butter . . . a guilty pleasure she picked up after observing her canine stepsisters Sasha and Maggie begging for the scrumptious treat.

Ever watchful, the motion of my hand lifting the knife from butter to bread caused a vocalization from Midnight as she anticipated the morning ritual. Breakfast.

Midnight nudged me affectionately as I slid the buttered bread onto a plate, placing it on the kitchen table. Like a puma, she leapt counter-to-counter to reach her destination. Spoiled, she managed to position herself front and center, hoping I wouldn't notice the dogs.

As she sat pretty for her treat, Midnight displayed "Her Majesty" pink bling—complete with crown—that jingled from a magenta-and-gray collar, appropriately compliment-ing her coal-black fur. Plumped, primped, properly postured and with lips pursed, she stood prepared to pounce on the slice of pumpernickel if it was not offered to her—pronto!

Midnight wasn't persnickety about her carbohydrates, be it rye bread, scone, muffin or sourdough. It was impera-tive, however, the bread be generously dripping with butter, the sweet-cream kind, salted or unsalted. I fared better than to feed Midnight margarine or a cheap imitation—she knew the difference.

A scrumptious morsel laid before Midnight was in-spected briefly by Her Highness to ensure the entire portion was covered with her favorite fatty substance. As she daintily crunched the savory sustenance, the butter's exquisite qual-ity melted with acceptance on her taste buds. She waited for another. And another. When her tummy was full, Midnight sashayed to her throne—the soft, quilted comforter of the guest bed, where she sought solitude.

Midnight is the epitome of a queen. And what the Queen wants, the Queen gets.

And the Queen likes her bread and butter.

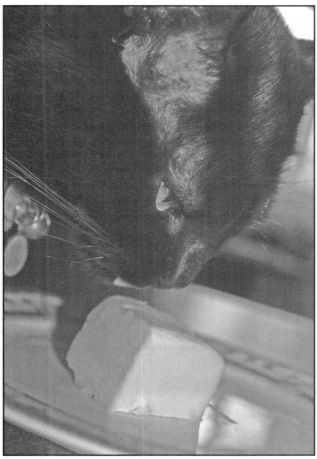

The Queen eating her butter

Sleepless in Culver City

by
Mary McGrath

We have three cats in our household. I like animals better than people, and if I had my way, I'd probably have more than a dozen. That is, assuming someone other than me managed the cat box and kibble chores while I kicked back and enjoyed the zoo of activity.

But that's not going to happen. Thus, I'm the one in charge of kitty stuff at my home in Southern California. It just sort of fell into my lap and there it stayed.

Having three cats can be a bit of a challenge, especially when it comes to coordinating the space on the bed. Our cats love to sleep with my husband and me. In particular, they love to sleep near me, and I often find myself in some sort of pretzel position around 2 A.M., wondering if I'll be able to recover my posture by morning.

It starts with our eldest, Sparky, a spunky Siamese who wedges himself between us when we first go to bed. Perhaps he's dividing the turf so hubby and I have equal shares of the mattress. But I think Sparky simply thinks he's a surrogate boyfriend. During the night, the cat will inch closer to me, as if he's ready to make out. Sparky's face is so close to mine that his whiskers wake me up.

The second arrival is our youngest, Holly, a fluffy rag-doll/Siamese mix. Holly insists on occupying most of the foot of the bed, making it impossible for me to stretch out. In the middle of the night, she's usually sprawled in one of those flying positions—you know, where all limbs are out-stretched. From the looks of her, she should probably take up skydiving.

The third cat is our Milly, a stubborn calico who insists on dominating my pillow. I suspect she used to work in a hat shop in another lifetime, as she plops right next to my head and begins mewing and crawling all over me around 4:30 A.M. This makes it hard if I've had my usual bout of insomnia, but I usually end up getting up anyway. Unfortunately, it's a battle I'm always going to lose.

Some people will shoo cats off the bed if they get in the way. But since our cats are all rescue cats, I can't bear to do this, for fear they will develop additional psychological problems beyond the trauma they endured before we rescued them. What if one of the cats suddenly felt dejected by me and began wanting to see a therapist? I can hear it now . . .

"My owner doesn't love me anymore," she'd begin, while the therapist takes copious notes. "She used to let me sleep on her head, and now I have to sleep at the foot of the bed. I really miss smelling her shampoo and face cream. I don't know if I can sleep by myself. Besides, I'm afraid of spiders—and thunderstorms." The doctor would prescribe a handful of cat treats, and I'd get a bill for $272.

I could try buying each its own Posturepedic bed, but

we have no room and I don't feel like stubbing my toe in the middle of the night. I've even thought of converting the den into some sort of cattery, but I know the three of them would revolt. Our male would probably spray all over my computer, Milly would pick at her fur until there was enough on the floor to knit a sweater and Holly would simply barf by the door so I'd be certain to step in it when I enter the room. Naw, that's not going to work.

I know I would have been a terrible parent if I'd had children. All they'd have to do is look at me with those sorrowful eyes and I'd be pulling out $20 bills for them, giving them chocolate cake 24/7, and letting them skip school whenever they had a stomachache or wanted to sleep in. My children would live at home with me until they were 52, and I'd allow it.

Such is the life of this cat owner—a cat owner who averages only four hours sleep a night.

Holly

Milly

Elmo's Lesson

by
Sioux Roslawski

"Just looking" at the Humane Society is dangerous for me. If I'm in a mall, I can shop all day and not buy a single thing. Cruising from store to store, wandering down the aisles, I'm quite skilled at spending hours on a window-shopping spree and coming back home empty-handed. And I'm happy.

Perusing the cages and runs at the Humane Society is another story. I've never left without finding a bargain. Unlike a dress or a T-shirt that—once bought—needs little maintenance beyond laundering, the purchases I've found at the pound could get quite expensive. And although I loved some of my well-worn pairs of jeans, I've never been loved back by any of them. No sweatshirt can curl up on my pillow at night and keep my shoulders warm. No blouse does figure eights around my feet over an opened can of tuna. Nope—never happens.

Our family was in the early stages of getting a new pet. We had two kids—our daughter Virginia, who was in the fourth grade, and our son Ian, who was in preschool. We had a dog, and our older cat was going to be approaching the cranky and crotchety stage in a couple of years. A younger feline, we figured, would help us along when the senior one passed away. Going to our local shelter would prod us into brainstorming what we were looking for—once we got truly serious, that is. Cats are fun to observe, and we had nothing else to do on this particular Sunday afternoon. It seemed like a marvelous idea.

Kittens were cute, but we figured their constant playfulness would probably aggravate the cat we already had, so we didn't even glance into the kitten room once we arrived at the shelter. Entering the adult cat section, we all headed in different directions, drawn by a twitching tail we saw or a melancholy meow we heard.

And there were some gorgeous cats. Longhaired ones with fur the color of smoke, their golden eyes glittering like jewels. Siamese cats with eyes the color of the ocean, their cream bodies contrasting with their gray ears and paws. Cuddly-looking calicoes. We would call out to each other to come look at a cat we'd found, and each one we saw made us squeal even more. OK, my husband was not squealing or shrieking, but he trailed behind us in a good-natured way.

As we continued to peek into the cages, we saw a tan tabby, which had very faint white stripes blended in with fur the color of a watered-down orange Dreamsicle. He sat at the entrance of his wire home, looking at us. While most of the other cats pranced or preened or napped, he simply sat there.

We learned the cat was a seven-month-old male who had been picked up as a stray from a neighboring rural county. His personality didn't scream out at us and his looks were not striking in the least, but we were curious. In our quest to become more-informed shoppers, we wanted to get a better look at him. The attendant removed the cat from his cage for us.

Once we held him, we were hooked. He pulled us in with his purring, and this cat could purr like a motorboat. He also settled into our arms like a baby. We rocked him, and he snuggled up contentedly, as if he was the ball of love we were looking for.

With plaintive puppy-dog eyes from Virginia and re-lentless pleas from Ian, we gave in. Our window-shopping had resulted in a purchase. Our family was now going to include a tan tabby. Since Ian was glued to *Sesame Street* every afternoon, we named the cat "Elmo."

As soon as we brought him home, we discovered Elmo was one sick kitty—at both ends. He threw up several times and was plagued by diarrhea. After a trip to the vet and a couple of weeks' worth of runny poop, we got his digestive system regulated. We forgot what kind of havoc his stray days had wreaked on him, but Elmo—he *never* forgot.

Our newest feline family member was determined to never be hungry again. No matter how much dry food we put out, Elmo would empty the bowl. Since we were feeding two kitties, it was difficult to ration his food intake strictly. Putting out just a little resulted in desperate meows from our tan fellow, begging for more.

Overeating was not a concern while Elmo was active and young. During his first few years with us, he developed a jiggly belly. Running across the room after Megan, our top cat, Elmo's stomach would rock to and fro, but it was smaller than a tennis ball and not a big deal. I had a bit of a pooched-out tummy my-self, so I couldn't get too upset with him over his overindulgence.

I gorged on ice cream and brownies. And chocolate chip cookies. And mashed potatoes. And . . . well, you get the idea. I felt a tad hypocritical when I tried to make drastic cutbacks on Elmo's food. He was still able to play and romp around and he was still able to keep himself clean, so the bit of extra weight didn't seem to be too much of a hindrance.

As the years progressed, Elmo's pounds piled on. The tennis ball was now the size of a softball. Elmo's normal-sized head was mismatched to his butterball body. He was still playful, but had to twist himself into a furry pretzel—like a contortionist—in order to clean his back legs.

Another thing Elmo never forgot was being free. Our cats were indoor kitties—there was no way we'd risk one being hit by a car or attacked by a loose dog, so we never allowed them outside. Most likely Elmo felt imprisoned, as if he had a life sentence, after having roamed freely for his first seven months. But that's what we wanted for him—life—so we didn't give in to his attempts to escape.

Once a month or so, Elmo would slip out the door. Many times he'd be crouching by the front door or the kitchen door, waiting, but we'd see him and put a foot out to block him as we left. Occasionally, we'd be too slow and he'd make a break for it. With his tennis ball-sized belly, he could streak across the grass with such speed that we'd have to dive after him. As Elmo's weight increased, however, his speed decreased, and the most he could muster was a trot when he made his getaway. We would walk—leisurely—to catch up with him and take him back inside.

Eventually, Elmo got to be the size of a ham. A whole ham. His head stayed small, but his body was alarmingly large. Elmo looked like a sumo wrestler with a pinhead. He had more rolls than my dinner table at Thanksgiving, and he could no longer keep himself clean. And yet, he still yearned to be free.

One night, when one of us let the dog out, Elmo slipped out as well. We didn't discover his absence until it was too late. We called for him. We shook a box of cat treats to tempt him back. We even drove around the neighborhood, hoping to catch sight of him, but it was all in vain. Elmo had eluded his jailers and was loose.

For the first few days, we held onto hope. We thought he might be in a neighbor's yard napping in the bushes and reveling in his freedom. Or, since he was such a cuddler, we assured ourselves that he was taken in by a cat lover and was safe and comfortable in someone else's house.

After more than a week with no sign of him, we started worrying. The cat across the street—Tigger—roamed freely, and he was a scrapper. Part of Tigger's ear had been bitten off in a fight, and Elmo—who had no front claws—would be defenseless against a dog or a tough cat like Tigger. Our 10-year-old tan fellow also was not used to cars. Would he know to avoid the road when headlights came his way? We weren't sure.

When Elmo had been missing for three and a half weeks, we resigned ourselves to the fact that he wasn't coming back. We watched for his body and were relieved a pile of something on the road didn't turn out to be his lifeless form.

One evening, I took the trashcans out to the street. As I was heading back inside, I heard something.

Meow.

It was quiet. Faint. I tried to convince myself I had actually heard something.

It sounded like Elmo, and yet it didn't. It was much softer

than his normal voice, so I figured it was a stray cat that had wandered into our yard. But I called out anyway.

"Elmo?"

I got a weak meow in response, which made me stride across the dark yard in the direction of the sound. What I found surprised me.

It was Elmo, but a thinner Elmo. A new and improved Elmo. I scooped him up and carried him into the house, alternately chastising him and smothering him with kisses.

No matter how many times we asked him to tell us, Elmo never divulged what had happened while he was away. We got no details as to where he had slept or what kind of adventures he'd had or what food he had been able to snag.

But from that point on, we called Elmo's 25 days away from home his trip to the "Fat Farm." And finally, he had learned at least one lesson, because he never tried to escape again.

Elmo after his visit to the Fat Farm

Becoming the Purr-fect Cat Guardian

by
Ernie Witham

The other day, I sat down to have a heart-to-heart discussion with Sam, my cat. Excuse me—I mean Sam "the" cat.

See, there is a huge pet movement going on and I have just gotten the scoop. According to the national coalition group "Friends and Lovers of Every Animal (FLEA)," we are no longer supposed to consider ourselves owners of our pets. Instead, we are now supposed to consider ourselves their guardians.

At first I thought they were kidding. I mean anyone who has ever lived with a cat knows there is no owning them. Cats are the most independent creatures in the world. Sam comes and goes as he pleases. Stays out all hours of the night. Hangs out with other cats from the "Hood," cats we know very little about.

Still, I guess the idea is that if we consider ourselves guardians rather than owners, we might take more responsibility for our actions. I hoped that was true because I now had the responsibility to take Sam to the veterinarian's office for a couple of days while they tented our house for termites. I was feeling a bit skittish.

"Sam," I said, getting down on all fours to establish equality, "we have to talk."

Sam looked at me for a minute then batted his catnip-laced rubber ball toward me.

"Maybe later," I said. "This is a sober discussion."

I began to pace, which, I might add, is not all that easy when you are down on all fours.

"Sam, there comes a time in every guardian's life . . ." I hesitated, so the full impact of this new term had time to sink in, ". . . when he must make tough decisions, kind of like when Jon and Odie had to put Garfield on a diet."

Sam stopped licking himself and glared at me.

"No. I'm not putting you on a diet."

Sam began licking again.

"I'm taking you to the . . . that is . . . on a little vacation. Yeah, that's it."

Twenty minutes later, we were at the vet's office.

"Welcome, Mr. Witham," the veterinary assistant said. "I need to ask you a few questions before Sam sees the doctor."

"Can you please refer to the doctor as the 'resort facilitator'?" I whispered to her.

"Say what?"

"Sam doesn't like the V-E-T," I said.

She sighed then continued. "How long has it been since

Sam has been to . . . our resort?"

"I don't know exactly, but I think Bill Clinton was president."

"No way! How old is he?"

"Fifteen."

She looked at me in disbelief. "So, he's a senior cat." She wrote this down.

Oh, no. I knew what that meant. Sam would now end up on every major senior-cat mailing list in the country. He'd start receiving *Modern Caturity* magazine. Get those endless membership solicitations from the AARC (American Association of Retired Cats). Brochures would start showing up from feline tourist bureaus throughout the country: "Spend those last few lives 'owner-free' in Miami, where the days are warm and the mice are slow. Dye your fur and be a kitten again. Have your claws buffed every day. Join our bird-watching group."

And what would happen when Sam found out that I had been listing myself as his owner all these years, like he was a piece of property? Would he secure legal counsel? Seek reparations? What kind of reparation did a cat want?

"Mr. Witham . . ."

"Huh?"

"You're ranting, Mr. Witham, and you are frightening Sam, not to mention me. Now, if you'll just sign this admittance form . . ."

I grabbed the cardboard pet carrier. "I've changed my mind. I'm going to find a hotel that takes cats. Then Sam and I are going to share a can of fancy albacore in spring water. We're going to drink real cream and lay around on uncovered furniture, shedding together. I may even buy Sam a new collar. That'll show those fleas!"

I headed for the door. Just as I was leaving, another guy came in with his cat.

"Hi, I'm Big Lou," he said gruffly to the assistant. "And dis is Boss Cat. And I need you ta 'splain to him that I'm cool wid da guardian thing. Oh, and he don't want no shots, neither."

She sighed again. "Welcome to the 'resort,'" she said to Boss Cat. "And to the longest day of my life."

Sam relaxing in the backyard

CHAPTER TWO

Where the Wild Cats Are

From cute to crazy!

Cat-awampus

by
Mike McHugh

Never have I lived in the middle of a war zone, until now. And it's not fun. Our house is a war theater, and it makes a battleship seem like *The Love Boat*.

It all started when we got a new cat. It was not my idea. My wife always wanted ours to be a two-cat household, presumably so they could keep each other company. I, for one, never saw the logic in this, but I didn't get a vote.

A few months ago, the older of our two cats finally kicked the bucket. In cat years, she was older than all of the members of the Rolling Stones put together. It was her time. This left our younger cat—Angel—the sole feline. She was very happy about her new situation, being the undisputed queen over her dominion.

The house is not ours, believe it or not. We are merely Angel's slaves—there to feed her and clean her litter box.

Still, all was right and at peace in our little world.

But my wife has never been one to leave well enough alone. She insisted that we had to get another cat to replace the one that had passed. I warned her that bringing another cat into our house would upset the balance of power, with potential to touch off a powder keg.

She wouldn't listen. "Don't worry," she insisted, "we've got a big enough house. They'll each stake out their own territory and establish a peaceful coexistence, just like before."

I had to admit she was right on this. Angel did let our older cat have the pantry where her food bowl was—at least when it wasn't feeding time—and Angel got the rest of the house.

Then along came my editor, Lauren, who was the ultimate enabler to the cat-addicted. Lauren totally sold my wife on a cat named "Bertha." It was a difficult task, but easier than selling flood insurance during a hurricane warning.

"Lauren told me the cat is very intelligent," my wife said. "She listens to Beethoven and can meow in Latin."

I was not impressed. "Ask her if she has one that listens to Willie Nelson and talks football," I answered. Still, my opinion on the matter was not important.

Angel, to put it mildly, was even less enthusiastic. The moment Bertha came through the door, she gave me a look that I could only interpret as saying, "Don't expect me to share my food with that fur ball. Let her forage for lizards."

My wife interpreted it by saying, "Look, she's curious."

"Oh," I replied, "is that what it means when her tail gets puffed up to the size of a chimney brush?"

When the post office processed Bertha's change of address and the first issue of *Feline of Fortune* appeared in our mailbox, I knew it was going to be trouble.

Bertha would never be content with the border being drawn across the pantry threshold. No, she had designs so grand as to make Napoleon's ambitions seem like a property-line dispute between neighbors. And Angel, whose main ambition in life was to emulate a sack of potatoes, she saw as no threat at all.

Now the tables were turned. Angel's territory was currently reduced to the small space under the china cabinet in the dining room, a place she could barely squeeze into with her Jabba the Hutt-like girth, but she did. This was a testament to the amazing things a cat can do when desperate.

Meanwhile, Bertha proudly assumed position on Angel's former throne—the arm of my recliner in the den. Tufts of cat fur littered the dining room floor, evidence of Angel's futile attempts to regain ground.

Now, I can't approach my recliner without rousing Bertha's ire, probably because I have tried to take Angel's side in the conflict. I felt I owed it to her for all those times she loyally sat at my feet while I played guitar, something no human has ever dared to attempt. I have often rushed to her defense with the ultimate ballistic anti-cat weapon—a spray bottle. It may contain only water, but to a cat, this is worse than any chemical weapon ever conceived by overzealous Middle East dictators. But, I can't be there for her at all times, and so such victories are short-lived.

Things at our house are still unsettled. Bertha still views

me as the enemy. I see no chance of making peace with her, particularly since I can't play any Beethoven on my guitar. And even though I'm Catholic, I don't know a word of Latin.

I tried calling the United Nations to see if they could spare a few peacekeepers, but I was told all their people were tied up in the Congo or some such place. It's a shame, because I have a feeling that the conflict here is about to spill over the border. Yesterday, I caught Bertha on the dining room table studying a map of the neighbors' yard.

What bothers me most about it is that I don't think there's enough room underneath my china cabinet for their Rottweiler.

Bertha and
Angel (in box)

The She Devil

by
Debra Ayers Brown

I was prepared for a hurricane. I even had a fireplace in my Charleston bungalow in case coastal South Carolina experienced a freak ice storm. But I wasn't ready for a She Devil.

The saga started on day one when Boyfriend surprised me with a tiny white-and-black Persian kitten. It stretched and yawned in the palm of his hand while he explained the male cat had had his shots but was too young to be neutered.

"All he needs is love," he said.

I was touched because Boyfriend wasn't usually so thoughtful.

Everything seemed fine until Christopher Cat raced around the house like a banshee, shrieking and writhing in pain. The vet informed me my four-month-old Christopher Cat was a Chrissy—and she was in heat.

A girl? I was stunned. I made arrangements to bring her back to be spayed.

On spay day, I looked everywhere for Christopher Cat—oops, Chrissy—nicknamed "CC" for short. She wasn't in any of her favorite spots. I finally heard a faint *mew* from her high perch on the drapery rod. But no treat or sweet talk enticed her to come down. Balancing on a chair, I grabbed the hissing cat and shoved her into the carrying case.

"She's still spirited, long after her hiss-terectomy," I joked to Mom when my parents visited a few months later. We looked for CC, but she was nowhere to be found.

Soon I heard "Holy God!" from the kitchen. I knew what had happened. CC enjoyed two things: knocking down everything in her path and using her sharp claws to climb. Sure enough, Dad stood stock-still and bug-eyed with a 7-pound cat clinging to his back. But CC wasn't done. She rounded the top of his shoulder, kneading, giving an, "I'm drawing blood" massage then turned to flash us a wicked smile.

Boyfriend suggested CC might suffer from a crisis of gender. So I explained it wasn't unusual to mistake a female cat for a male if you weren't trained. Uh-uhh. She wasn't having it. The She Devil wanted revenge.

Through the years, CC toppled crystal vases, clawed the couch, attacked my calves and howled at night. She seemed determined to torment me for what I had done to her.

But when Mom and Dad visited again, Mom said CC dashed to the front window every day before my normal arrival time to wait for me. How could I resist her?

After a 10-day business trip in a colder-than-usual

January, I rushed to get CC from boarding and then home. I'd worried about her the entire time. And I couldn't wait to see my birthday present, a remodeled bathroom courtesy of my self-professed handyman Boyfriend. But my only bathroom was in shambles with black plastic for the outside wall. No shower. No heat. Welcome home.

The next morning, I had to wash my hair before work. So I placed a space heater on the counter and cranked it up to high. I scrunched my body in the tub to lean my head back under the running water. From that awkward position, I noticed CC pounce onto the counter, moving closer to the heater. I gasped. With one swipe, the heater flew through the air, and I raised my arm, deflecting it. The heater thudded against the floor. My heart pounded as CC looked at me with big, gold, unapologetic eyes. I trembled, realizing I could have been fried in the tub by a She Devil.

I suffered no more murder attempts, but CC continued to test my patience. Every time I'd swear enough was enough, she'd snuggle up to me and purr. She remained my companion long after Boyfriend cheated, and I moved on.

Even now, I've forgotten most things about Boyfriend, including his name. But the feisty little feline remained close to my heart. When a new cat entered my life, I searched for signs of a reincarnated Christopher Cat turned Chrissy turned CC. It wouldn't be the first time she'd surprised me. I doubted it'd be the last, considering nine lives and her devilish chutzpah. Let's face it—even a tarnished halo wouldn't last long on a She Devil.

Cats Gone Wild

by
Myron Kukla

I used to be a normal person with a normal life. These days, I spend my spare time moving quietly through the woods with a blanket over my head, trying to sneak up on wild animals.

No, I haven't lost my mind. I simply have two cats that are driving me to strange activities as I try to trap them for their required spaying visit at the vet.

I received Princess and Duchess from a farmer. He said they would be good mousers, and I needed just that to keep mice and small critters out of my garage after my Collie—Jo—died last summer.

When I got Princess and Duchess home and let them loose, they disappeared under the steps to the garage. They didn't want to have anything to do with me, even though I brought them food and water and little cat toys with bells on them. They took my gifts without as much as a whiskered

"Thank you."

I have to admit, I've never owned cats before and all I can say is they are not like dogs. You feed a dog. If you give it water and scratch it behind the ear once in a while, it will be your friend for life. A dog will follow you anywhere with total trust, including trips to the vet to be altered. When you try to do the same with a cat, it says, "Who is this guy? He thinks we owe him our reproductive parts in exchange for a little canned tuna? He's crazy if he believes he's going to get us to the vet like he did that dog."

To make matters worse, after a week I noticed the cats where looking daily to me for more food, even though their dinner dishes were cleaned every night. I thought maybe they were fattening up for winter, but one night, as I drove into the garage, I spotted the real culprit. It was a large gray-and-black raccoon, happily munching on their food while the cats watched from a safe distance.

Well, I know enough about raccoons to realize that once they find a nightly meal-stop like mine, they keep coming back. So now not only did I have cats to catch, but also a big hungry raccoon prowling my yard and garage.

I decided to solve two problems at one time by renting a "humane animal trap." I figured I'd set it, baited, outside the garage in the woods and either catch the cats or the raccoon.

The first morning after I set the trap, I went outside and saw an animal moving in it. But something wasn't right—the animal was black with a long white stripe down its back. I had caught a skunk! My yard was becoming a regular wild-animal preserve.

I figured I'd solve my new skunk problem by calling

the wild animal unit of the sheriff's department to get rid of it. Much to my surprise, I found there is no such thing as the wild animal unit in the sheriff's department, although I think there should be one.

So, I called up Mike's Nuisance Animal Control. Mike advised me that, 1) he would pick up my skunk and release it far away in the woods for a BIG fee, or 2) I could be a brave grown-up person and release it myself.

"A skunk will just walk away once you open the trap door," Mike told me. "It's not like a wild raccoon, which sometimes will turn and attack you when you let it out."

Lesson learned: a skunk is better than a raccoon in a cage, but not as good as two female cats that need to go to the vet.

I opted to be a grown-up. Mike advised me that best way to get rid of the skunk was to approach the cage with a blanket in front of me, and then cover the cage with it, open the door and walk away. The skunk, he said, wouldn't spray me because it would think I was a blanket.

Thus, we return to the beginning of my story. On that sunny afternoon, I took the good quilt off our bed and headed outside to release the skunk. Then I thought better of it, putting the good quilt back and getting an old blanket from the basement.

Walking toward the trap with the blanket over my head, I spoke these words in a quiet reassuring tone. "Hi there, Mr. or Ms. Skunk. I'm just a blanket walking through the woods. There's no need to fear me, for I am a friendly blanket that wants to release you from your trap and not the bad human who put you there who you might want to spray and make all stinky."

And it worked. I covered the trap without being sprayed,

opened the door and ran like crazy back to my house. And I waited for the skunk to come out. And I waited and waited. I finally went back and peeked into the cage to see what was going on—the skunk was curled up into a ball, sleeping. It had found a safe, warm place to live and liked it.

I wasn't worried. I figured that eventually the skunk would have to come out for food and water. Later that night, I looked into the trap with a flashlight. The skunk was still there. Not only there, but in the process of building a skunk nest, complete with microwave and color television.

But the critter made a mistake when it left the cage to arrange to have cable installed. While it was away, I dismantled the trap and skunk nest, keeping the microwave and color television for myself.

The whole experience has taught me a wonderful lesson. From now on, I'm staying in the house and leaving the wild animals to themselves in the woods. As for the cats, they can just drive themselves to the vet.

Myron in disguise

Pulling Her Own Strings

by

Cappy Hall Rearick

At three o'clock yesterday morning, I was awakened by a loud bumping and scraping sound coming from the family room. It scared me into the middle of next week.

"Babe!" I shook my husband awake. "There's an intruder in the house! Get the baseball bat."

"You're dreaming," he muttered as he rolled over. "I was having a good one until you woke me up. Go back to sleep and don't wake me unless it's for ham and eggs."

I shook him again.

"Oh, for heaven's sake. Did I stutter?" Babe slid out of bed, grumbling, switched on the light and nearly blinded me. When the scraping noise started again, he actually stopped bitching long enough to listen. He grabbed the bat, and that's when a thought hit me: *Do I really want Babe facing down an intruder with a kid's baseball bat while he is wearing polka-dot boxers?*

Oh hell, any port in the storm. "Hurry!" I whispered a

yell. "If it's a would-be Charlie Manson, he's probably out there choosing which wall to write on with our blood!"

"That's some imagination you've got, girl." Babe walked out of the bedroom, flicked on the den light and searched the area. The only thing he saw was the rear end of our cat—Sophie Sorrowful—as she darted under the sofa. Assuming the cat was somehow responsible for the noises, he reached under there to pull her out.

When Babe's hand began to feel for the cat in her hiding place, Sophie Sorrowful darted out the other side and began a frenzied promenade around the room. Dragging and bouncing my grandson's forgotten yo-yo over the tile floor, she unwittingly repeated the bumping and scraping sounds that woke me up and scared me silly.

It was a wee little yo-yo, not much bigger than a 50-cent piece. My grandson had won it as a prize at an arcade. It was such a precious prize that he didn't bother to take it home with him, leaving it instead on the floor where Sophie Sorrowful found it.

Bump. Bump. Boiiiiinnnnnggg!

Babe cussed like a sailor, gave chase and finally grabbed the cat by the scruff of her neck. Holding her close to his sleep-encrusted eyes, Babe saw that Sophie Sorrowful had swallowed all but the yo-yo itself and about 6 inches of the string.

His first thought was to cut off the wooden yo-yo hanging out of her mouth, which would allow Sophie Sorrowful to swallow *all* of the string and eventually poop it back out. After only a nanosecond, he thought better about it, thank goodness. It was a long string and well . . . it could take days, maybe even weeks before the end of that string ever saw the underbelly of a litter box.

He tugged on the yo-yo ever so gently.

"EEOOWWOOEE!" shrieked Sophie Sorrowful.

Then holding her as firmly as anyone could possibly hold a squirming, screaming, terrified cat, Babe gave the yo-yo a really hard yank.

Sophie Sorrowful let out another "EEOOWWOOEE!" which set off the burglar alarm and sent me hopping out from under my warm covers faster than a speeding bullet. When I got into the den, Babe was standing in the middle of the floor in those silly polka-dot boxers, looking stupid. He was holding the yo-yo up with the tips of two of his fingers, its yucky-looking string dangling underneath. Both he and Sophie Sorrowful were taking turns gagging.

Sophie Sorrowful was so thankful to have been delivered from a strange and eerie fate that Babe became her personal Don Quixote. Skillfully dodging Babe's size 11 brogans, she dogs his footsteps like a bloodhound. Any day now, I expect to hear her bark, but I'm pretty sure she won't be doing any more yo-yo tricks.

On Duty

by
Carol Commons-Brosowske

Cledean Jones and I are both the best of friends and co-workers. She was always the first one in the office, but one day, she wasn't there when I arrived. Naturally, I began to worry when I didn't hear from her. I called her several times, leaving several messages, all of which went unanswered. It was three hours before I finally received word from Cledean. That's when I learned about her harrowing experience.

Just as Cledean was leaving for work, she noticed her patio door was open. Neither she nor her husband ever used that door—it was always locked. She panicked and immediately phoned her husband. He assured her he had not used the door and to get out of the house and call 911.

Once outside, Cledean called 911 and told the dispatch operator she believed there was an intruder in the house. Within minutes, three police cars came barreling up the street. One parked in front and two screeched to a halt in the back-alley driveway. They moved Cledean to a safe area then headed inside the house with guns drawn.

"DON'T SHOOT MY CAT!" Cledean screamed to them several times as they were entering the home. "Oh, and by the way, she's not exactly friendly!" she added as they were going inside, but she was not sure they heard her warning.

Cledean was more worried about her cat Missy than she was a possible burglar. Missy—a gorgeous cat with a jet-black and chocolate-striped shiny coat—had become Cledean's baby when the couple had become empty nesters many years earlier.

Missy is the sweetest and most gentle cat to Cledean and her husband and they adored her. It was obvious that Missy only had eyes for her human parents. Other people or pets run for the hills when they see that cat coming. She can be vicious and will attack without motive, scratching, biting and hissing at anyone.

I've often tried to make friends with Missy, but she will not have any of it. I've always assumed it was because she smelled my dogs on me. Usually pets of any kind like me, but this one cannot be won over by my gentle intentions. Missy is known far and wide as "The Cat From Hell." Her vet even calls her by that name, and he is a true cat lover. Missy has been his patient since she was five weeks old.

Cledean, standing out by the police car, was frantic, waiting for word about any intruder and her beautiful kitty. Finally, two police officers came running out of the house, screaming like little girls.

"WHOA! There's a wild cat after us! No one can get past her. She is one hell of an attack cat, for sure," the lead officer—Sarge—told Cledean as he approached her.

"We've searched every inch of your home. There's no one in there except a stray wild cat that probably wandered in through the open door. You'd better call animal control—this one is mean," added Officer Bruce.

"She attacked all three of us," Sarge said, pointing to his fellow officers. That's when he realized only one officer was standing next to him.

"Hey, where's Joe?" Sarge asked Office Bruce.

"I dunno, I thought he was behind me when that malicious cat was chasing us."

Suddenly, Joe came charging out of the house, looking behind him every step of the way. He was as pale as a ghost.

"Whew! That was close," Joe said to his fellow officers and Cledean. Trying hard to catch his breath, Joe added, "That is one mad cat in there."

"That's my cat. You didn't hurt her, did you?" Cledean asked in a concerned tone.

The officers looked at Cledean in bewilderment, as if they couldn't believe the cat was a pet.

"Ah, no, ma'am. She's not hurt and there were no intruders found. I actually wish there had been instead of dealing with your wild-eyed, 30-pound black she-devil in there. No offense, ma'am," Joe said.

"None taken," replied Cledean, but she could hardly contain her laughter.

"Holy crap," said Patrolman Bruce, wiping his brow. "She pounced, hissed and spat at all three of us. She then chased us out of the bedroom."

These three burly and armed policemen were terrified of a big old pussycat. They had run out of the bedroom and through the house screaming as if they were all on fire. That's when Cledean realized that they must have awakened the Satan-like cat from her morning nap. That was a big mistake, and she told them so.

"As long as you have her, ain't no way any strangers are going in there," Officer Bruce said as he got into his patrol car.

The other two policemen walked together back to their cars in the alley, discussing the ordeal. Cledean overheard their conversation.

"Stop that scratching, Joe. You're making yourself all red."

"I can't help it, Sarge. I'm allergic to cats."

Before the officers left, they told Cledean that, without a doubt, there really was an attempted home invasion earlier that morning at Cledean's house. They assumed the person got just inside the door before being confronted by Missy. The suspect was frightened away by the demon cat.

For Cledeans' last birthday, I gave her a sign which is placed outside of her home: "Attack Cat On Duty." Those words have never been truer. After all, it's only fair to warn these would-be burglars of what lurks on the other side of the door. If they only knew, I'm sure they would try another house to conduct their shenanigans.

Missy is now 13 years old and continues to live a happy life. She is content, but always on guard duty, 24/7. No need for a Doberman or a Rottweiler when you have a kitty like Missy.

A terrified Carol (left) and Cledean with Missy

My Cat is a Junkie

by
Sheila Moss

It must have been a stroke of genius when my grandson named her "Frisky." I have to admit, the current problem is at least partly my fault, so I can't in good conscious say too much. Nevertheless, a normal cat would not behave this way. Frisky, of course, is not a normal cat.

It all started when I was watching that program *My Cat from Hell* on television. The animal behaviorist said that cats want something green to nibble on and suggested providing them with a planter of cat grass. My mistake was when I decided to plant catnip instead of grass. All cats like catnip, don't they?

I should have known. I once planted some catnip in my herb garden. Cats from miles around came to visit. It became such a nuisance after a while that I pulled it up. But being from the mint family, the catnip was hard to get rid of—it was just like a weed. It took years to eradicate the catnip completely.

This time, however, I planted the catnip in a pot so it could be contained. In only a few days, the seed sprouted and plants quickly grew to be several inches tall. Either the plants didn't like the container or it was the unseasonably hot weather, but the plants wilted and couldn't be revived. I knew that cats liked dried catnip, too, so I stripped the dry leaves from the plants, put them in a plastic baggie and left the kitty weed in the kitchen.

Frisky was especially naughty the next morning, knocking a jigsaw puzzle that my grandchildren had been working on for days off the table and onto the floor. I thought it was only Frisky being frisky.

However, it was a bit more. Frisky was nipping on the catnip. She had jumped to the kitchen counter—where she is not allowed—and had chewed the plastic bag open. She then apparently sniffed the weed until she was high. I found out too late that catnip is actually pretty potent. Some people call it cat marijuana. I had no idea that cats can go crazy over it.

Felines are affected by the smell of the oil in catnip, which is similar to eucalyptus. When the leaves are crushed, even more of the scent is released. Cats usually react by rolling around and becoming playful. It is supposedly not harmful.

But for Frisky, the catnip sent her over the moon. She had scattered her vice all over the kitchen. She knocked the cat food off the counter and turned over a large container of kitchen utensils. She then staggered to the kitchen basin, knocking the dish soap bottle into the sink. From there, she smacked a package of donuts onto the floor.

I suppose, in her imbibed state, Frisky thought she could fly. I know this because she leaped to the very top of the kitchen cabinets and rearranged all the decorative baskets there. When I investigated the commotion, I found Frisky on top of the refrigerator, denying everything.

In case you are wondering, catnip only affects cats. It does not have the same effect on people. I looked it up to be sure. It will only make you sleepy. So, if you are heading to the garden shop to buy catnip seeds right now, forget about it.

I caught Frisky on the kitchen counter again this morning, undoubtedly looking for her fix. She was busted.

That's when I realized I was harboring a feline drug addict. As I said in the beginning, I am an enabler for planting catnip in the first place. I had no idea it would cause all this.

I really don't want my cat to become a pothead. If you happen to hear of a catnip rehab or 12-step program for cats, please let me know. Frisky is going on the wagon, and if I have my say, she won't be falling off anytime soon.

Frisky taking
a break

Thieves and Vandals

by
Harriet Cooper

I was in the den reading when a crash reverberated through the house. I put my book down and sighed. "Damn cats. What have they broken this time?"

I told myself that if I was wrong—if a tree had fallen against the house or a driver had lost control of his car and crashed into my front window—I would apologize to the cats. But when it comes to crashing noises, there's usually a paw involved.

A quick search of the downstairs showed nothing out of place or in pieces on the floor. I headed upstairs. Delaying the obvious, I checked my office and guest bedroom before heading into my bedroom. Or should I say the "cats' room," since it's their favorite place and where they do the most damage?

I was only a few steps in when I noticed two things. One, my new mirror was no longer leaning against the wall on top of my dresser. Two, an inch or so of gray tail was sticking out from under my bed.

I closed my eyes and counted to 10. When I opened my eyes, nothing had changed. Words that would have had my mother washing my mouth out with soap escaped my lips. The tail moved further under the bed.

"Sammy!" I screeched. "What the hell have you done?"

Sammy didn't answer. Her handiwork spoke for her. Loudly and in pieces. Many pieces.

Muttering under my breath, I went downstairs to get the vacuum. When I came back, the tip of her nose was poking out from under the bed.

"How did you do that? You weigh what? Ten pounds. The mirror weighs at least twice, maybe three times that. How did you knock it off the dresser when I, a woman who weighs, well, let's not get into specific numbers here, let's just say a woman who weighs considerably more than 10 pounds, could barely lift it?"

Sammy still didn't answer.

I contemplated the mess on the rug between the dresser and my bed. A friend was coming over that weekend to help me hang the mirror. Guess that wouldn't be necessary.

For one small cat, Sammy has cut a wide path of destruction through my house by pushing a variety of knick-knacks off shelves, tables and dressers. There's the unicorn that is now missing its horn, the vase with a crack in it, the piggy bank that will never hold coins again, the glass bowl I inherited from my grandmother, the figurines . . .

To be honest, I never liked the figurines, but if anyone was going to break them, it should have been me. Not my cat.

I crouched down next to the bed. "Damn it, Sammy, why can't you, just for once, use your feline super powers for good instead of evil? You know, be more of a Supercat who tries to save the world rather than a Lex Luther double who tries to destroy it—beginning with my house."

Sammy meowed softly, but remained safely hidden.

Since I was already near the floor, I began to pick up the largest broken pieces. "Crap." I licked a bead of blood from my finger, and then dropped the glass into the garbage can. A few more followed.

Before I was done, Tiger, my older cat, poked her head into the room.

"Scat," I said, waving my hands at her, "there's broken glass. I don't need a vet bill on top of this." Either Tiger understood or, more likely, she was uninterested. Unless I'm covered in eau de tuna, Tiger is rarely interested in anything I do or say.

Spying Sammy under the bed, Tiger hissed at her, promising future punishment, not for breaking the mirror but simply for existing within Tiger's realm. As Tiger sauntered out, I sighed yet again. Broken mirror. Sibling rivalry. What next? I wondered.

I deposited the last of the large chunks in the garbage can and grabbed the vacuum. "Sammy, vacuum time. Run for your life."

A nose, some whiskers and part of one eye peered out at me. "Come on, Sammy. You have one minute to come out from under the bed before I start vacuuming."

Sammy hesitated, so I turned on the machine. A blur of gray streaked across the room and out the door—faster than a speeding bullet.

For the next few minutes, I concentrated on the sound of crunching glass. I mentally added the cost of the mirror to Sammy's mounting tab, which was close to the $400 mark.

All this for a "free" cat. Some deal.

A few days after the incident, I was at the local framing store with the empty frame, getting an estimate on replacing the mirror. The framer did some calculations and came up with a price only slightly less than what I had paid for the original.

"Damn cat," I muttered.

He grinned. "I know what you mean. I have two. All I can say is that they're all thieves and vandals. Yup, thieves and vandals, every last one of them."

I laughed. "I know. If my cats complain they come from a broken home . . ."

". . . it's because they've broken it," he finished.

The next week, my friend came over to help me hang the mirror. After she left, I checked my reflection. In the bottom left-hand corner, a small gray face peered at me.

I turned around. Sammy was sitting on the bed. I joined her and she curled up on my chest, purring. "Not so fast," I said, as I tickled her under her chin. "You are not forgiven. The cost of the mirror is coming out of your allowance. I haven't forgotten about the unicorn either. Or the vase, the piggy bank, the bowl . . ."

I broke off in mid-sentence as her purrs slipped into soft, ladylike snores. My $400 cat and rising. As I continued to pet her, I remembered something my father used to say to me. "I wouldn't sell you for a million dollars or buy another one just like you for a buck."

Staring down at my very own thief and vandal, I knew exactly what he meant.

Top Dog

by
Nancy Julien Kopp

My daughter Karen and her fiancé Steve spent lots of time making wedding plans and deciding how to blend their two homes into one. Furniture and cooking pans were the least of their concerns—they needed to figure out how to get three pets to live harmoniously in one house.

Karen and her male cat, Ming, shared a townhouse and that big white cat liked life just as it was. When Steve became a regular visitor, Ming accepted this other man in his mistress's life, but only a little at a time. He kept a wary eye on Steve, who spent more and more time with Karen.

Pet introductions were a critical step for my daughter and future son-in-law's nuptial bliss. Karen described the meeting to me during a lengthy phone conversation, telling me how Steve had arrived at her townhouse with his two brindle Boxers in tow. I listened to her tale, fearing what the end of the story might be.

Max and Riley—the Boxers—were big, muscular dogs and a bit fierce looking, even though they were usually pretty calm canines. Excited and with their sides heaving, the dogs confronted Ming while the humans held their breath. Barking and snarling, Max and Riley advanced.

Ming fled to the kitchen and leaped onto the countertop, with Karen, Steve and the dogs close behind. The cat paced while eyeing those two devil dogs. The attack cat was ready to rumble.

In no time at all, Ming flew at them, claws out, and with a fierce expression on his usually tranquil face. Ming's screeches and the dogs' barking filled the small kitchen for an instant. Add Steve and Karen's voices trying to calm their individual pets, and chaos reigned.

When Max and Riley charged in their counterattack, Ming retreated to a place on the counter where he knew the dogs could not reach him, even though they could still see him. Back arched and hissing, Ming waited just out of the intruders' reach.

Their night of terror didn't last long. Steve gathered up his two big dogs and headed home, leaving a worried Karen and a still-angry cat alone.

Karen told me she had a talk with Ming after Steve and the dogs left, and no doubt, Steve reasoned with Max and Riley on the ride home. The five of them were going to live together and they would have to learn to get along. This engaged couple didn't know it then, but they were training to be parents. Handling kids would be a piece of cake if they managed to get the three pets to live together peacefully.

Weeks later, I spent a weekend with the newlyweds and their menagerie. I'd always been more partial to dogs, but

Ming had worked his way into my heart long before. He often curled up next to me whenever I visited.

That afternoon, Max and Riley stationed themselves in front of the sofa, on both sides of my legs, chins on the cushions, slobber included. Ming Kitty snuggled closer to me, not making a sound, but if looks could kill, we'd have been digging two big holes in the backyard for those sweet dogs.

Later that evening, the dogs were standing in the kitchen, hoping for a scrap or two from dinner, when I noticed Ming saunter by them. Without missing a beat, he whacked one of the dogs on the snout with his paw then kept right on walking. Max and Riley both looked a bit bewildered, but left the cat alone. It was obvious that Ming had established his spot on the family tree, and it was several branches higher than that of the dogs. It may have been the first time a large white cat had claimed the title of "Top Dog."

Another year passed and the first baby joined the family—she was named "Jordan." After I did all the silly things a new grandmother is wont to do when meeting a grandchild, I left the new parents at the hospital and went to their house to feed the animals and spend the night with them, as we'd prearranged weeks earlier. Those three pets had learned to tolerate one another, even though Ming occasionally used the swat-on-the-nose method to keep the dogs in line. I wondered how they were going to accept the newest family member who would be coming home the next day.

I shouldn't have worried. They all loved Jordan, and as she grew, she fit right in with the three of them. Once she started to crawl, she chased Ming daily, with her eye on his long white tail. Luckily, he was faster than she was, but I think he enjoyed the game as much as she did. Max and Riley lay on the floor watching, tongues hanging out. I knew they were cheering her on from the sidelines. If they could speak, they'd have been hollering, "Go, Jordan! Get that tail!"

The family lived in harmony, with Ming reminding Max and Riley that he ruled with the occasional nose swipe. It wasn't a hard swipe—it was more like Ming wanted to remind the dogs that they were guests in his house and they'd better not start any trouble. He'd never admit that he'd come to like those two guys.

Max was the first of the trio to pass on. But Riley still had Ming, and the cat seemed to sense his canine brother's grief. They kept one another company and became good buddies. When Karen and Steve were at work and Jordan was at day care, those two probably had a few good laughs together about the time they first met. That night of terror resulted in a long friendship, even though Ming Kitty still wore the crown. Yep, he'd always be Top Dog of the feline world.

Ming

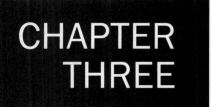

What's New Pussycat?

Lessons learned from our feline friends.

Two and a Half Cats

by
Janine V. Talbot

For several years, we have had a unique pet situation in our home. Our neighbors and good friends have a winter home in Florida, and we have taken care of their cat—Midnight—in their absence.

In the beginning, it was only for a couple of weeks at a time, so we catered to the cat. Each morning one of us—whoever couldn't get out of the house fast enough to avoid being volunteered by default—would cross the street to our neighbors' house and let Midnight out in the morning. Toward evening, we called her back in, often using the sound of her dry-food container being shaken.

That was fine for the short term, since Midnight was usually cooperative and willing to head back to the old homestead, even if it meant being alone at night. I believe she probably relished the solitude. She had plenty of food and water, and the queen-size bed was finally hers alone.

A couple of years into this arrangement, our neighbors began staying in Florida for several months. We needed an alternative plan for cat duty. Remembering to run across the street to let her out when we were often already leaving the house, late for school or work, and trudging over to let her back into her house each night, just got to be too much. Attempting to make her an indoor cat in her own home would have required cement walls and metal curtains. So we decided to introduce Midnight to her personal cat co-op—our house.

For the first couple of winters, it would be as much as a week before Midnight would take to this new arrangement, which required her to appear at our door on her own when we called her. She preferred to sit saucily on her own front porch—even in the middle of a snowstorm—and wait for us to dutifully track her down. When this happened, her favorite game was to leap off the porch the second we climbed those icy steps to the neighbors' front door. Eventually, we would snatch the little fur ball up and carry her into our house, where she would skirt the walls like a SWAT team member and ninja crawl her way down the basement steps.

Somewhere, still undiscovered by us—and no amount of bribery would suffice in unveiling her secret—Midnight had found a super-secret hiding place. In the middle of the night, when no person or creature was up to witness this, she cautiously slipped out from concealment and scoffed down a ration of food. She would then slink back to her niche and remain there until morning. Well, her version of morning. We'll get into that shortly.

As time went on, Midnight adjusted to the long-term arrangement as if she had made a reservation with us for the winter months. Magically, she would appear at our door on the same day the neighbors left for warmer weather. Midnight even tolerated the shaggy shadow of our dog Cubby and the playful pounce of Sophie the acrobat cat, as well as the disdain of our eldest cat—Reeses.

Midnight entered our home with the expectation that her schedule was "The Schedule." Our version of dawn and a cat's version of dawn are—as we discovered—often in very different time zones. One of us needed to adjust to the fact that there is no 4:30 A.M. in our house, which was the hour her owner—also referred to as her normal home staff—released this 5-pound mountain lion to the great outdoors.

I always thought Midnight had the cutest little cry, similar to the first sound an infant makes upon waking. It's a soft warning that things can get messy if someone doesn't respond soon. When it started no less than an hour before anyone needed to be up, Midnight's adorable little wail became nails on a chalkboard. It was as if she had shoved a siren into her tiny mouth. Her screeches continued until one of us finally broke, lunging after the little feline tornado as she whipped down the hall to the kitchen door, confident her next destination was outside. Well played, Midnight. Well played.

Eventually we learned not to heed her catcall until we were good and ready, which was anywhere from 15 minutes to two hours from when she first sounded her alarm. After a couple of years of constant retraining each time she moved back to her winter residence, she learned to wait semi-quietly. Losing patience with us,

Midnight has been known to prod us by hiking across a stomach or back with her sharp nails or working her way up to a face, where she asks, "Why aren't you up yet?"

By early spring, Midnight's long, elegant fur develops a texture similar to something that has met an eggbeater and glue. Globs of her beautiful mane have to be combed, cut and occasionally shaved off. When you see my husband don a heavy pair of jeans, two long-sleeved shirts and welding gloves, you know Midnight must be trapped in a bedroom somewhere, just waiting for a chance to take on him and the comb.

When it's all over, my poor, beaten spouse will reappear, red-faced and sweating profusely, holding up clumps of black fur in triumph. Midnight flees from the scene silently, promising to seek revenge when her assailant least expects it.

Midnight has on occasion pulled an all-nighter, especially when spring weather comes on, but we don't worry as much as we used to about the foxes or coyotes that sometimes slink through our neighborhood in search of a snack. This cat has mad cloaking skills. Usually around the time we are crawling toward the coffee pot, she will appear on our porch and wait for one of us to remember that she has modified the schedule. Once let in and gently chided, she will pop over to her food dish for a quick breakfast before demanding to be let back outside within five minutes.

Last winter, we lost our much-loved oldest cat Reeses to health issues. It has become just one and a half cats since that time, but there has been discussion—more like not-so-subtle hinting—about adding another furry friend to the fray. This way, we can keep our court jester, Sophie, company during those summer months when Midnight crosses the street to peace and quiet.

Adding a half cat to the menagerie and hairball collection has been amusing, entertaining, and, on occasion, exhausting. But when Midnight climbs up onto my shoulder and wraps her little paws around my neck as a request for me to pet her, that loud, contented purr is nearly impossible to resist . . . once I remove her claws from my skin.

For as long as Midnight will winter at her personal cat co-op, we'll leave the light on for her. And she will continue to ignore it and honor us with her presence in her own good time.

Midnight

Meow-thering

by
Julie Hatcher

As a teenager, baby-sitting didn't appeal to me. However, my fascination with cats drew me into the whole mothering phenomenon.

Mese, a Siamese kitten I adopted after graduating from high school, taught me a little about "meow-thering," which is a close second to mothering. Let's just say he dared me to think outside the box, the "litter box," that is.

Fortunately, working full time and leaving a new kitten at home alone didn't set off any alarms to Social Services, because I would've been in big trouble. I guess I didn't read the book, *A New Mother's Guide to Raising Kittens*, under the heading "Beware of Poisonous Novelty Items."

One evening after work, I returned to my apartment to find Mese half-dazed and sprawled out on the carpeted floor. Beside him lay a small black snake, partially eaten and regurgitated in a puddle of cat spew!

Mese appeared more cross-eyed than a Siamese cat

should. Determined to stand on his own, he stepped forward and drunkenly ran into the wall, collapsing. *Bing!* A light bulb illuminated in my new-mother noggin. Although unintentional, I had given Mese a toxic toy—a rubber snake. The proverbial "Mr. Yuck" symbol for poison control must have escaped me.

Frantic, I called a veterinarian. Explaining my kitten's state of distress, the vet simply instructed me to pour milk in a dish and offer it to Mese, thus letting Mother Nature take its course. Shortly after he drank the milk, Mese began to walk surefooted and his turquoise eyes appeared less crossed. Meow-thering had its challenges, but it taught me a valuable lesson—to develop hunting tactics for cat-safe toys. Otherwise, milk may do the trick.

When Mese was two years old—or age 14 in human years—I faced his rebellious teenage stage. He often attempted to sneak out of the apartment. I insisted he remain strictly an inside cat, but he tested my parental controls. A door left ajar for a split second would beckon him to clamber into the wild blue yonder. Of course, my first command, "No, Mese, the world is a scary place," only taunted him. So, with car keys in hand, I clanged them like bells to startle him into submission when I had to go outside. It worked like a charm . . . for a while.

Mese, a clever opportunist, learned consistency was the key to success. One day, he fell beneath my radar and slinked through the sliver of space between the door and the doorframe. Like a dandelion seed in the wind, he wafted into the great wide-open. I had failed as a mother. My juvenile delinquent, both declawed and defenseless, had left me a tearful, nervous wreck. I searched through bushes and underneath cars, and I posted flyers at every doorstep.

Two weeks passed, and like any mother of a cat worth her whiskers, I held onto faith. After returning home one night, on the walk between the car and the apartment door, I chanced a summoning by jingling the once-enchanted car keys.

"Meow," a cat answered.

Shaking the brass keys again, I listened for the magical catcall. It came again, allowing me to single out the meowing bush. Pulling back the shrubbery, I couldn't believe my eyes. It was Mese!

I gently tweezed him through the bramble. Harboring my humbled cat within the warmth of a mother's arms, the two of us returned to our four walls of civilization. My feline boy, dehydrated and famished, held his head high and stepped over to his food dish to satisfy his thirst and starvation. Perhaps he had to find out for himself that independence is a bear and hissing snakes will attack. But through it all, he learned that Mama's keys were the way to safety. Conversely, I learned to never give up on runaways and to look for the bush with the silver whining.

Meow-thering has taught me a little about cat courting. As a mature adult cat, Mese was responsible for wooing a female gray tabby, probably luring her with cat-eyed winks through the window. She literally knocked at the door on Christmas Eve, with the dragging of a paw. This feline version of Scarlet O'Hara sashayed her way into Mese's heart and humble abode. She demanded her claim with all the grace of a winged cat. Giving her both the name Angel and a new home, I essentially betrothed Mese to her. And the wedding vow would've read, "To provide all the cuddling and licking, for better or for worse, until their hearts content. Amen."

Unfortunately, I thwarted any opportunity to have a

conversation about the birds and the bees with my boy. I hoped the subject would be an innate cat trait—however, I'm not sure Mese ever figured out what procreation was all about. On occasion, he saddled up in his attempt to ride Angel like a racehorse, but completely on top, not from behind. She must have been a pillar of patience to Mese's half-witted effort. As a spectator, it reminded me of a skit from *The Carol Burnett Show*, when Tim Conway readied to fire a cannonball and Harvey Korman yelled, "Fire!" The ball never made it out of the chute. Mese had afforded me another meowthering lesson—to be prepared to laugh my hiney off over his bedroom shenanigans.

Meow-thering not only taught me that raising a cat was perfect practice for mothering, but it had other perks, too. No one ever said, "Oh, what a bad mother you are for giving your cat a toxic play snake." And luckily, I was never interrogated by a police officer on the suspicious disappearance of my rebellious teenage cat. Furthermore, having been helped by a humane organization, I chose sterility over fertility for my catty boy, just in case he ever really fired that cannonball.

Angel (left) and Mese

Cat Therapy

by

Julaina Kleist-Corwin

When April comes around each year and daylight saving time starts, the birds chirp loudly enough to wake me at 5 A.M. They seem to chat to one another, as if the night of silence was too long.

I was happy they were happy, but I needed more hours of sleep. The night had been long for me, too. I couldn't stop rehearsing what I had to say to a staff member the next day at work. *It doesn't matter what I tell her—she won't like it,* I assured myself.

I yawned, rose and gave thanks to the universe that author Rachel Carson's prediction of a silent spring hadn't happened yet. I shuddered at her description of a pesticide-impacted world unfit for all life, a world without the birds' songs. I opened the window and whistled a reveille bugle call back at them. "Sorry for wishing you would stop," I added.

A detour on my way to the shower led me into the spare bedroom, where my garment-bagged power suits hung in the closet. *What I wear today must emphasize my authority.*

I tiptoed past the massage table that I had set up in the center of the room for once-a-week acupressure sessions. The practitioner appreciated the convenience of having a table at my home for her to use.

My cat—SuSa—valued it, too. She had left the bed during the night, probably tired of my tossing and turning. I found her curled up on the blanket-covered table. At first glance, I wondered which end was her head in that oval mound of gray fur. She stirred at the sound of the closet door opening. One golden eye peeked over her tail to check me out.

"Good morning, SuSa."

The small cat made a *meumph* response. Not a real meow, but a *meumph*. In slow motion, her body uncoiled, she rose on her long slender legs, and then teetered for a moment when her mouth expanded into a big yawn. Her flexible body stiffened into a slow, deep stretch with her chest brushing the table. *Why can't I manage that position in Yoga class?*

After my shower and dressing, I felt good in my perfect-fitting professional suit. SuSa raced me into the kitchen, where she wrapped her body against my leg. I like to think of her leg-wrap as a kitty hug, but it was her way of reminding me to get her food. When I bought my house, the sellers asked if I'd take their cat since it would be hard to travel with her across the country. Sight unseen, I agreed. When I moved in and saw her, a Blue Russian breed, I loved her immediately and imagined her as a temple cat guarding the house and me.

I put the cat food into her dish and said, "I'm sorry I was restless last night and disturbed your sleep." She lifted her head from her breakfast to look at me. She licked her lips and her eyes seemed to say, "What?" I remembered that animals lived in present time—she probably forgave me hours ago.

We finished our breakfast in silence. I envisioned my assistant's face when I told her she was no longer needed at our school and that she would receive two weeks' severance pay. She had been late and absent too many times. *Will her expression be contrite or angry? Well, I know she certainly won't be surprised.* She knew of my concern about her unreliability, since we had talked about it many times, but she hadn't changed. I'd hire the on-call substitute to take her place.

My trembling hands caused my coffee to spill over the edge of the cup. I didn't like to affect someone's livelihood, but the assistant's actions put a burden on other staff members and me. Plus, her absence disrupted our students who liked consistency. I dumped the rest of my coffee into the sink and wiped the spilled drops off the placemat.

SuSa's loud meow told me she was no longer a sleepy cat—she was ready for the day. After making eye contact, she hurried, with tail straight up, to the patio door. Her ears perked and her tail swished. She looked at me again and let out a loud, impatient *meow*.

I opened the patio door, and she paused a moment, letting her olfactory sense test the scene. Apparently satisfied, she took her usual leap over the bristled doormat and sauntered to the potted plant placed diagonally from the door. She sniffed the flowered stems as if the plant consumed her interest. However, the position of her ears showed she was alert for anything unusual at a distance, as well.

Like me, SuSa could multitask. While I taught a full

class of students, I was also the school's unofficial adminis-
trator of its satellite campus. Immediate multiple challenges
filled most of my days.

SuSa was my therapist. She took good care of me. When
I was sick with a cold, she'd lay near my chest. If I had aching
hamstrings from too much exercise, she'd sleep by my thighs.
The time I had a bout with food poisoning, she settled down
next to my stomach. If I came home upset from work, she'd
sit on my lap and purr. Her dreamy eyes took me to a serene
world without words, without stress. Her approach to the
outdoors taught me to slow down and enjoy nature while
preparing for the unexpected.

The plant passed her scrutiny and she moved to the center of the patio where she sat on her hind legs, twitching
the tip of her tail. Her front legs stood straight in front of
her body like a gray adaptation of an Egyptian cat statue as
she examined her yard. The morning sunshine made her fur
glisten like dew on the leaves of a fern. Her head rotated 180
degrees to see if I was still at the door, watching her. I blew
her a kiss.

Then a bird rustled in the bushes on the hill. SuSa rose
on all fours and stood, frozen at full attention. Her ears re-
shaped into two pyramid-like antennae and pivoted on top
of her head to pick up every sound. She slinked toward the
retaining wall, leapt to the top of it, and remained in an
arched position. Then she glided into a wide radius to approach the bushes from behind the noise. She wasn't going
to let that bird leave the yard without a fright attack.

SuSa was right. Fright isn't always a negative. It's a built-
in survival mechanism. My assistant's loss of her position
could result in a fright attack, which might make her a better

employee on her next job. I sighed and took in a breath of the flower-scented air. SuSa confirmed my decision to fire my assistant.

SuSa's form disappeared into the shadows of the bushes. I closed the patio door and wished the bird good luck. I hoped it would continue to join its bird friends and keep twittering nonstop in the mornings. Noisy, happy spring times and cat therapy—what more did I need?

SuSa

Heat of the Moment

by

Angela McKeown

I nearly had to explain a different meaning to "in the heat of the moment" to my 10-year-old son Eric. And it was all Mona's fault.

Our foster cat, Mona, was rescued with her two kittens. Mother cats are predisposed to view male cats as predators, so when Mona arrived at our house, our male cat Mushu was her instant enemy. He knew better than to rumble with a hormonal momma cat, so one hiss from her had him cowering in a corner.

Mona's kittens found families to adopt them. When a mother cat first realizes her kittens have inexplicably disappeared, she frantically searches and pathetically howls for them. Mona was no exception. Once her kittens went to their forever homes, she wailed and whined and rummaged through the house trying to find them. After a few days, Mona gave up on the quest to find her offspring and returned to normal. Temporarily.

A few days later, Mona started howling again. This time, however, it had nothing to do with her protective or nurturing instinct, but rather a different kind of primal instinct. Mona was in heat. *Moan-a* was a good name for her.

Mushu suddenly went from predator to prey in Mona's eyes. It took Mushu a while to adjust to this new relationship. He was Mona's punching bag for weeks when her kittens were still around, but now she was bellying up to the bar saying, "Hey, good looking. Buy me a glass of milk?" She definitely wanted to be his Dairy Queen. As she pursued him incessantly, his terrified eyes were as big as saucers. They would have gone well with that glass of milk.

Since Mushu had already been neutered, he just stared at Mona in a *cat*atonic state in response to her propositions. Mona's advances toward him turned out to be the *cat*alyst for a very uncomfortable conversation with Eric—a conversation littered with many an awkward pause. And some awkward paws, as well.

"I feel so sorry for Mona. She's still crying and looking for her babies," said Eric.

"Mm-hmm," I muttered, holding back a giggle. *She is looking for something all right. But she is saying "come here baby" for a different reason,* I thought to myself.

"Mona has been a lot more playful since her kittens left. She tries to play with Mushu all the time. She crouches down with her butt up in the air, like she's going to pounce on him," continued Eric.

"Mm-hmm," I chuckled. *I haven't heard it referred to as "pouncing" before, but we can call it that. However, she wants to be the pounce-ee. And she's probably the type to hiss and tell.*

"Mushu doesn't seem like he wants to play, though," Eric mused.

I choked out another "mm-hmm," shaking from my feeble attempts to disguise my laughter. *Mushu doesn't have the balls to play with Mona. Litter-ally.*

OK, my actual response was just the "mm-hmm" part. But I wanted to say the rest. Oh, how I wanted to say the rest! It would have been the perfect opportunity to sing a new version of *Mony Mony* using Mona's name, including the "special" lyrics typically sung at a frat party, of course. Better judgment prevailed though, and I kept my thoughts in my head and walked away. Humming.

I pondered whether this incident was the *purr*fect segue into a conversation about the feline facts of life, but ultimately decided that the birds and the bees—kitty style— could wait. I chose to let a pounce be just a pounce for a little longer.

*Cat*astrophe averted.

Mushu

A Cat Named Cat

by
Susan Whitley Peters

Cat lay on the floor, looking peaceful, only the tip of his tail moving, waiting for the unsuspecting bare foot to move within striking distance. I was wearing sandals, although steel-toed boots would have been better. Cat was not declawed.

"It would hurt him," Mom told me. "Besides, he only grabs at you if you tease him."

"Or walk in front of him," I said. "And look what he's done to the bottom of your sofa."

"That was when he was a kitten," Mom said. "He doesn't do that anymore."

No, I thought, *now he can sharpen his claws on people!*

When my three-year-old granddaughter Cheyenne came to visit for the first time, she asked the obvious question: "Why do you call him 'Cat'?"

"That's his name," answered Mom. "Hey, Cat," she said.

Cat glanced up at her from the corner of the sofa.

"See? He knows his name."

Cheyenne thought this was the funniest thing in the world. "Cat!" she shrieked. "Here, Cat!" She made a grab, but Cat—no fool—swiped at her, claws out.

"He tried to scratch me!"

"He doesn't like strangers touching him," Mom told her. "He'll be nice when he gets used to you."

"Like when you're a teenager," I muttered.

Mom had adopted Cat as a kitten from the shelter. Now seven years old, he was a hefty gray-and-black-striped tom, white on the belly, with a suspicious nature and what I thought of as "cat schizophrenia." Mom admitted as much.

"Watch out when he has that look in his eye," Mom would say. "He gets wild."

Now, had one of her six kids "gotten wild," Mom would have straightened the offender out with a few well-placed smacks of a hairbrush. I used to think my brothers got preferential treatment, but now I had no doubt who was her favorite.

Once, between teaching assignments, I called Mom and told her I'd be coming up to stay for a couple of weeks.

"You'll have to sleep on the couch," she said.

"What about the back bedroom?"

"Cat likes to sleep on the bed in there."

"So the cat gets the bed, and I get the couch?"

"He's here more than you are."

I couldn't argue with that. Fortunately, Mom's couch was long and comfortable. The first night I was there, Cat prowled around, sizing me up as I spread out the sheets and fluffed the pillow.

"Don't even think about it," I growled.

"Don't be mean to Cat," Mom called from her bedroom. "Just put him in his room and close the door."

His room?! I picked him up carefully—Cat had a way of knowing what you were intending, somewhat like Mom with us when we were young—and carried him back to his kingdom. "Nice Cat," I muttered, dumping him on the double bed. *Spoiled evil creature*, I thought, closing the door.

Mom and Cat had a routine. In the morning, she fed him before fixing her coffee and oatmeal. During the day, he might sit on the windowsill and study the birds at the feeder, or he and Mom would lie on the sofa together, watching the soaps. In the evening, Mom would lure him back to his room with a treat. She never let him in her room. He got in once and hid under the bed. While she was asleep, Cat jumped up and made himself comfortable. Mom awoke gasping for air—with Cat's tail in her face and the rest of him across her neck, he had become a heavy feline muffler.

One day I got the call I dreaded: Mom was in the hospital, having trouble breathing. It was summer, and since I wasn't teaching, I went up to stay for a few weeks. As soon as I saw her, she asked about Cat.

"He's fine," I said. "In fact, we're getting along great." An exaggeration.

Mom frowned. "I better get out soon or he'll forget about me." Two days later, having bullied the nurses and her doctor, she came home.

Now she had a walker, and the television volume was louder. It was obvious to me that she couldn't live on her own, but when I brought up the subject, she absolutely refused to consider assisted living. My mother, never a patient person, was getting ornery with age. I wondered if that would be me in 20 years. If so, I pitied my daughter.

When Cat, who was getting old and crotchety himself, refused to go into his room, Mom could no longer pick him up and carry him. I was in the kitchen, having a late night snack, when I heard her talking, first wheedling and then angry, and finally with a kind of sob, "Bad Cat. Why won't you go to bed?"

I found her sitting on her bed, trying to catch her breath. "He's too heavy for me," she sighed. "Usually he goes right in, but sometimes he won't mind." I picked up Cat, who was lurking in the hallway, and settled him for the night.

A few days later, I had to call an ambulance. Mom was having breathing problems again and a terrible pain in her back. She would be in the hospital for a while.

The next day, I was in her bedroom, alone, when Cat ran in and jumped on her bed. He crouched and kneaded the rumpled sheets with his front paws. He looked up and meowed—not his usual growl, but softer, hesitant.

I picked him up, still careful of those claws, but he made no resistance. I carried him back to the kitchen and sat down with him in my lap.

He jumped down, ambled over to his food dish and looked up at me expectantly. I wondered, as I opened his tin of food, if Mom had a cat carrier—and maybe some steel-toed boots.

Dammit

by

Joyce Newman Scott

I guess it all started 30 years ago, with Dammit, a red-striped tabby that had crawled into my car engine on a bright sunny morning.

Back then, I was a flight attendant, working trips that flew back to back. That day, I was happy to be off from work to shop and catch up with my life on the ground. When I walked to my car in the parking lot of my condominium, I saw two young boys, who both looked about age 12, suspiciously hovering under my car. "There's a baby cat in your engine," one of the kids volunteered. He jabbed at the cat with a stick trying to get it to come out.

I commandeered his stick and nudged the kid out of the way. I crawled under the car to look. Sure enough, a sweet tiny face, mostly ears and whiskers, meowed at me. After much coaxing, I got the cat to climb out of the engine.

He was a little fuzzy ball with an innocent face, and he fit perfectly into the palm of my hand. I took him upstairs and pleaded with my roommate—Patty, a gorgeous blonde who was also a flight attendant—to let me keep him. Patty already had a docile calico named Happy, so it didn't take much to convince her.

Happy accepted my cat as if it were one of her own kittens, and within a few hours, both were racing around the apartment, playing dodge-cat and grooming each other. That's when I discovered that kittens have boundless energy . . . and enormous curiosity.

A few days later, I realized I still hadn't named my red tabby cat. I tried several attempts at names: "Red Cat," influenced by Hemmingway; "Frisky," "Purpuss" and even "Energy." But nothing seemed to fit his unique spirit.

The next day, as the cat pounced up onto the kitchen counter to watch me make breakfast, he followed me to an open cabinet and somehow managed to climb in. He looked at me as if to command more attention. When I ignored him, he hooked a paw onto one of my favorite china coffee cups and pushed it to the ground. As it shattered, I blurted out, "Get out of there, damn it!" That's when I realized that "Dammit the Cat" was an appropriate name.

Dammit lived up to his name. He would wake me bright and early every morning by dropping a peppermint candy, wrapped in cellophane, onto my bed and pushing it into my sleeping face. Usually exhausted and bleary-eyed after having flown all-nighters from San Francisco to Miami, I would throw the candy and Dammit would run after it. Bring it back. And want me to toss it again. Ugh!

To make him stop, I would get up and get him a bowl of food. While he was eating, I would return to my room and lock him out. Frustrated, Dammit would push a paw under the door and complain loudly. When that didn't work, he

would move to the couch and let me catch a few more bliss-ful winks. When I finally awoke, I would let him in, and he would nuzzle into my neck and lick my hair. I was just another big cat to him.

Eventually, I moved on with my life. I met a wonderful man named Tom, got married and moved out of my single-life condo and into a house in Coral Gables, Florida, where Dammit would sleep curled up on my shoulder at nights. We were one big happy family. But as Dammit hit his stride, he adopted a more assertive position in our household.

One night, Tom and I had planned to have a few people over for dinner. The table was set, chicken was stewing and the wine was uncorked. The only thing left to do was to put Dammit up for safekeeping—he was sleeping soundly on the couch, on his back, all four paws in the air.

Tom reached down and gently picked him up in his arms like a baby, cooing, "OK, Buddy, time to go into the bedroom." And that's when Dammit bit Tom, catching him squarely between both nostrils. Tom bled profusely for 20 minutes, just as guests were arriving. After cleaning the wound and administering ice, we continued with a great party. Tom didn't hold a grudge for the incident, but I'm not sure about Dammit.

Dammit finally passed on at 19 years of age from kidney failure. I would have done anything to prevent that from happening. I went into a four-week depression, moping around the house. I cried constantly. There was no consoling me. Nothing Tom could do to relieve my great sense of loss. Animals are family, and I had lost my only child.

After much protesting on my part, Tom dragged me to an "Adopt a Cat Weekend" at our local mall. About 20 cages filled the center of the shopping center. We circled around the cat cages as Tom pointed out all the cute and playful kittens. None of them tugged at my heart. I didn't care. I didn't want a replacement cat. I wanted Dammit back!

Tom finally gave up. He left me alone so that I could go back to my grieving, and he could tour the mall without guilt. A few minutes later, he appeared at my side and grabbed my hand, leading me across the room. "You've got to see this cat. This is the one," he said.

I stood in front of a small steel cage and stared at its contents. A gray-and-black tabby stuck her paw out and swatted at my hand as if to say, "Hey, you. Pay attention to me."

"That's a gray cat," I said. "Dammit was red."

"Give her some time," Tom urged.

I asked the woman who was running the show if I could hold her, and she agreed. She pulled out a folding chair for me, and I found a place in the corner. And in the middle of a shopping mall with people talking and children crying, this tiny creature curled up in my lap, rolled onto her back with four paws up in the air and purred. I held her as long as I could before deciding against taking her home. I apologized to the woman. "I'm just not ready yet."

The woman nodded and placed the cat back in her cage. "This is a very special cat," she said. "There's only one in 20. She should go to a home that loves her."

The cat, as if on cue, reached out again and tugged at my hand.

Is she playing me? I thought. "No, she's not the right one," I said, and we left.

We got as far as the parking lot when an overwhelming urge to go back came over me. Tom is a lawyer and not usually a patient person, but this time he agreed.

Back at the kitten's cage, I looked inside and searched my

soul. The tabby stroked against the bars, purring. I picked up one of the cat toys—a spongy ball—and tossed it into the cage. The cat ran for it, picked it up, brought it back and dropped it, waiting for approval. *Damn, she's fetching, acting just like Dammit did!*

I arranged with the woman who ran the Adopt-a-Cat function to let me take the cat home on a trial basis for three days. She agreed and produced a shoebox. We made tiny holes so that the kitten could breathe. As the woman handed me the kitten inside the box, she confided to me that she had turned down five other people earlier who wanted this very cat.

In the car, I slid the lid back for a quick look to see if she was OK. The cat rolled onto her back and purred and I stroked her belly the entire way home.

Within a few days, Tiger was running our house. She slept in our bed, right on the middle pillow between the two of us. She even fetched peppermint candies. And Tom and I argued about to whom the cat really belonged, and who she loved more. But there was no decision made and since then 14 more cats have shared the Newman Scott household. Thank you, Dammit.

Dammit

One Cat Shy of Crazy

by
Valerie D. Benko

A kitchen cupboard somewhere to my left squeaked open.

"Get out of there," I said, without looking up from my magazine.

The door shut with a thud. There was a loud, disapproving huff and the *clickety-clack* of toenails on the wooden floor as my tortoiseshell cat vacated the kitchen.

I continued reading until my thoughts were invaded again, this time by a crinkling plastic bag.

"Leave the potatoes alone!" I ordered, glancing at the perpetrator. This time, it was my calico—Buscemi—gnawing on the plastic bag the potatoes were in. She stopped for a moment, her green eyes gazing into mine, and then held my look as she resumed gnawing.

Aha! A challenge, I thought to myself.

My chair screeched as I slid it back from the table. Buscemi galloped out of the kitchen, did a flip in the hallway and mule-kicked the door. She disappeared into the living room and I heard her hiss at another cat.

I turned to walk back into the kitchen when a streak of fur slammed into my legs, knocking me into the wall.

"Archie!"

I was fed up. All I had wanted when I awoke before my usual time that morning was peace and quiet. Soon, I would be leaving on vacation, and I was looking forward to a week without my six cats. No cat fighting me for my cereal. No tail dipping carelessly into my coffee. No annoying scratching sound from a cat begging to be let into the bedroom when I'm sleeping in. No vomit to clean up or litter boxes to scoop. No cat hair on my clothes or toys in my shoes. It truly was going to be a vacation.

Yes, you might say, I'm one cat away from becoming crazy.

In the beginning, it was just my husband and me. The vacuum ran once a week and I dusted once a month. Guests always commented on how clean our house looked. I could participate in food day at work and not worry about being labeled the "pet-hair lady." And lint rollers? They didn't exist in our home.

There's an old saying that goes something like this: "Get a plant. If it lives, get a pet. If it lives, have a baby." Well, the plant died, but that didn't stop me from adopting two adorable kittens.

Lunk and Buscemi were sisters and couldn't have been more different. Lunk was needy. If she didn't receive constant attention, she would vomit on the floor. Buscemi was a sassy rebel who climbed the curtains and liked to kick things, like the closet door in the hallway, making it swing on its track.

I went from vacuuming once a week to twice a week and dusting two or three times a month instead of just once a month. Lint rollers became a staple and sleeping became a little less comfortable with one cat under the covers and the other between my legs.

Several years later, a pregnant stray showed up. She was friendly and looked a lot like a stegosaurus with spikey fur sticking up on her back. We made the mistake of feeding her, which meant she never left. As we spent months debating what to do with her, she gave birth on our porch to four kittens. We quickly moved Mama and her babies inside.

"We can't keep them," I told my husband as he sat in the game room, playing with the kittens. They were growing so fast and beginning to roam the house.

We listed them in the newspaper as "free to a good home" and two of the four found forever homes. We even found a home for Mama, who we had spayed. But the next day, the woman who took her returned to say that Mama had jumped out of her kitchen window and was gone.

The last two kittens—Archie and Petunia—hid whenever someone came to see them. Nothing we did, from locking them up to luring them with treats, made them visible. No one wanted to adopt a scaredy cat. And the humane society had no room, so we were stuck with them both.

Archie was the wrecking ball. If he could knock me out, he would. And he tries in the hallway, on the stairs . . . it doesn't matter where or when. On the other hand, Petunia is a loner, and we only hear from her when the entire cat food dish is missing one tiny speck of food. Suddenly, her alarm will go off. She wails like a siren, getting louder and louder, until I cover that missing spot with a little more food. Her dish is never empty.

One evening, my husband and I were eating dinner when we heard a faint *meow*.

"That sounds like Mama," I said, as I got up and peeked out of the window. "It is!"

Mama was staring up at the window, meowing. When she realized I was looking out, she twirled in circles, doing her version of a happy dance. It had been five months since she escaped her new owner's home. *Damn, I can't give away that cat now!* I opened the door and Mama ran in, curled up on a chair and slept for six hours straight.

And then there were five.

"We're at our limit," I announced to my husband. My house was being overrun by cats. I was being overrun by Archie. Lunk and Buscemi didn't like any of the new arrivals and picked fights where they could. My stress level was rising. And then Bugs came to stay.

Bugs was a tabby kitten abandoned on our porch by her mother. The frightened kitten sat vigilantly watching for her mother to come back, flinching at every sound. With the humane society full again, we scooped up the kitten and brought her in. She instantly befriended Archie and the other tabbies and put Lunk and Buscemi in their place. Slowly, the dynamics of the cat household changed. There was a new pint-sized sheriff in town.

But Bugs had her own annoying habits. Her food must be served in the downstairs bathroom—she won't eat anywhere else. To make her point, she will dance around my feet, nipping at my legs, until I oblige.

The vacuum cleaner and Pledge make daily appearances at our home. Sleeping in is a thing of the past. Socks are put on right before I walk out the door lest I step on a hidden hairball or puddle of puke. Snagged clothes are normal. I cringe any time someone asks me how many cats I have, but I have learned to answer, "one too many."

Yes, I need a vacation. Or a new house without cats.

Buscemi (left) and Lunk

It's Safer Down There

by
Lisa McManus Lange

Nosy Person: "Lisa, why are you limping?"

Sarcastic Lisa: "I tripped on a pinecone while feeding a toothless cat at 2:30 in the morning."

Truly, that's what happened.

Our neighbor went away on vacation during a long weekend, so she hired my son to feed her cat. It was only for the kitty's breakfast and dinner, so it shouldn't have been a problem.

So on the third night of "his" job, for some reason I was wide-awake at 2 A.M. After a trip to the washroom, hoping to remedy the non-sleeping issue, I went back to bed. The sandman was just about to have his way with me, when . . . *Oh, my God! I don't think the neighbor's cat was fed dinner!* I thought to myself.

I sifted through the sand in my brain, trying to remember if my son had gone over to feed the cat. True, it wasn't *my* job, and true, the cat *would* live until breakfast. But it would be *my* luck, during *our* watch, something horrible would happen to the cat.

Adding to my worry was that the poor thing had no teeth (for various medical reasons that aren't important here). I couldn't very well let it suffer any more than it already likely had—because of separation anxiety from her owners, strangers coming into her house and so forth.

By then it was 2:15 A.M. Realizing I would never get back to sleep worrying about the cat, I knew what I had to do. With a coat thrown over my pajamas and sporting a bed-head big enough to turn a raccoon into stone with one look, I headed to the neighbor's house, picking my way through the leaves. The extreme silence during that time of morning amplifies every sound, and I was sure that one wrong step on an extra-crunchy leaf would have our other neighbors calling 911.

Onward I plodded, down the lane, down some steps, finally arriving at the front door. Once inside the house, I was relieved to see the cat was safe and sound. Of course she was—she's a cat! Chastising myself for worrying needlessly, I fed her some pureed cat food then started my way back home. *Phew*, I thought. *Now I'll be able to go to sleep.*

I quietly picked my way up the outside steps, avoiding ear-piercing crunchy leaves at all cost. And then I stopped.

Oh, God. Did I lock their door?

I continued up a few more steps.

Um . . . hmmm. I can't remember. I scratched my head, fingers tangling in my scary bed-head hair.

I knew if I went home, I would never get back to sleep, worrying whether I had locked the door or not, even though I was sure I had locked it.

What if she got out? Aw, crap. I better go back and check. I'm awake anyways.

So back down the steps I went.

I stupidly stepped on some soft-looking leaves then stumbled and twisted my ankle on a pinecone hidden underneath said leaves. With arms, hair and nightgown flailing, a million thoughts raced through my head mid-stumble, all jumbled together in one long sentence:

What if I fall and as my body flails down the steps, I wake the neighbors and they see me in my pajamas and they call 911, fearing I am a crazy murderer, especially with my hair looking the way it does, and I'm not sure if I'm wearing clean underwear, and what about the cat, and what about and what about . . .OH, MY GOD! MY ANKLE REALLY HURTS!

I ended up in a heap of nightgown and hair at the bottom of the steps. After the sound of my ankle cracking and tearing finished echoing off the surrounding homes (I swear I saw someone's bedroom light come on), I hobbled my way down the rest of the steps and back to the neighbor's front door.

It was locked. *Lovely. Perfect. Great. And I should have been more worried about robbers than a cat being able to reach a doorknob to escape. Duh.*

Seeing all was well and feeling much better knowing the house was locked and the cat was fed, I hobbled home, my bed-head finally settling down. My shoes and coat were quietly thrown on the floor, and I made my way to the couch, desperate not to wake the rest of the family. I just needed peace, if only for a moment. Our own cat, which I barely had time to feed on a normal day, snuggled up against me. And, of course, she assumed it was feeding time, seeing as I was up.

I rolled my eyes, patted her on the head and then leaned

back on the couch and closed my eyes.

Then it started.

The throbbing. *Ba boom, ba boom, ba boom, ba boom.* That dull thud like a beating drum vibrated from my ankle through my leg, keeping me awake for most of the night. Or morning. Or whatever it was at that point—it really didn't matter.

I would later learn that my boy had, in fact, not fed the neighbor's cat dinner the night before, so my nocturnal antics were not completely unfounded. I would be grounding him for the rest of his life after all that anyways, so I was at peace.

But slave that I am to all kitties near and far, and to stop my own cat from pawing at my leg in silent signal, I gave in and made my way over to her kitty bowl for a midnight snack—for her, not for me. And, of course, I stumbled on a cat toy en route.

As I knocked back a few painkillers while my cat indulged in her own midnight snack, I contemplated curling up beside her on the floor. I figure it's safer down there.

Lisa and her cat, Sam

The Games
Felines Play

Ready . . . set . . . GO!

The Great Curtain Caper

by
Pat Wahler

Every home contains at least one item, prized beyond measure by its occupants. It's something to admire, fight for and treasure.

I found my Holy Grail of Housedom in a pair of curtains. The moment I saw those bronze basket-weave window panels, I knew they would be the perfect companion for the sliding glass doors in our great room. I carefully measured length and width as a smile lifted my lips. Decorating had never been my forte, but even I could see these curtains would be perfect.

I ordered the panels and a week later, they arrived in an extra-large mailing envelope. I tore it open and pulled out two tightly compressed fabric panels. A snapping shake unfolded each one. Bogey, my tiger-striped feline, immediately nosed his head inside the empty envelope. He scooted it across the floor, making the envelope look as if it had unexpectedly sprouted four legs.

"Can't you stay out of trouble for even five minutes?" I said, as I removed the envelope from his head.

Bogey meowed in response, no doubt informing me in cat-speak that such a question could only be rhetorical. I had no time to dicker with him. My husband had already hung the onyx-colored rod and I couldn't wait to see how the curtains looked in their place of honor. Wrinkles and all, I slid the panels onto the rod and stepped back to take a look.

A brief three-step happy dance followed. The curtains just touched the floor and were a lovely complement to the room. They made the entire area look warmer and perfectly finished. I'd made the right choice.

Bogey sauntered over to inspect the new addition. His tail stood straight up as he sniffed his way across the folds of fabric. Not 10 seconds later, his haunches tensed and he jumped at least 6 feet straight up. His claws latched securely to the curtain and he hung on. I couldn't help but notice how efficiently he had attached himself to the fabric. A utility lineman scaling a telephone pole could take a lesson from Bogey.

Finally, I found my voice and shrieked, "Bogey! Get off there now!"

Bogey released his hold and dropped neatly to the floor. I raced over to check the damage—he had punched several pin-sized holes into the fabric. My shoulders slumped.

Long ago, Bogey had demonstrated a penchant for knocking collectables to the floor. His behavior taught me to always ask myself one question before making a purchase: What will Bogey do to this? In many cases, the answer was enough to discourage me from buying an item. But curtains? It hadn't even occurred to me that curtains would present a problem.

Bogey meowed again and rubbed against my legs. I picked him up and stroked his head. He purred and my annoyance melted. Perhaps he'd been overly excited about seeing something new in the room. Cats tend to roll that way. Now that he'd gotten acquainted with them, surely he'd leave the panels alone.

But Bogey didn't lose interest. Any time I sat on the couch, he would leap and attach himself to the curtain. Then he'd turn his head like an owl and stare straight at me. The gauntlet had been thrown. I'd jump up and he'd drop to the floor and sprint away. It wasn't long before the new curtains had more tiny holes than a piece of Swiss cheese.

My husband ventured an observation. "He only does this when you're in the room. I think he's trying to get your goat. Why don't you just take the curtains down?"

"No way," I scoffed. "Besides, I have an idea."

I had read an article that said cats don't like sticky things. So I purchased clear contact paper and clothespins. The clothespins did a neat job of clamping the paper—sticky side out—over each curtain panel. While the result was eerily reminiscent of a plastic-covered couch found at Grandma's house, I didn't care. It worked. Bogey did not attack the curtains again, although he glared at me every time he walked past them. I felt smug about finding a simple solution to the problem.

A few weeks later, I watched as Bogey casually walked by the curtains, gazed toward the curtain rod, crouched and leaped. He cleared the contact paper with room to spare and hung from the top of the curtain. As soon as I yelled and moved toward him, he released his hold. I swear that cat had the most self-satisfied expression I'd ever seen on anyone's face.

Later that evening, Bogey jumped above the contact paper again. And again the next day. Now even bigger holes gaped in the fabric. My beautiful curtains began to droop as threads stretched and unraveled. Bogey's endless game of "Jump the Curtain" had clearly taken its toll.

Even the most fanatic soldier realizes when it's time to surrender. I took down my tattered curtains and gave them a dignified burial deep in our dumpster. I finally realized that no mere mortal would ever win in a power struggle with a cat, so my sliding glass doors remain naked to this day. It's much easier on my nerves to decorate around Bogey, although I'll never admit the truth to my friends. Instead, I describe my new style as "Modern." It's a simple decorating scheme that features only one risk-free accessory.

Cat hair.

Bogey and the infamous curtains

Mission Accomplished

by
Glady Martin

Before I retired, I worked with senior citizens as a private caregiver. I also worked at a home society center in Canada, the equivalent of a "senior nursing facility" in the United States.

At various times, I worked as a nurse's aide, counselor, hairdresser, cook, guide and driver. More importantly, I became a trusted friend and confidante to the tenants.

One year, there was an intruder who caused so much worry for all of us that we had to hire a professional security guard to work 24/7. But that wasn't our only intruder. We also had an animal intruder, who we called "Mr. Bear." That old bear loved the center's garbage container and couldn't get enough of it. The thought of a bear within their midst made the elderly skittish.

Eventually, when there were no further break-ins, the security guard was let go. That's when the center's management asked me if I wanted to earn some extra cash by patrolling the grounds each night from 10 P.M. until 1 A.M., in addition to working my regular day shift.

I had already tried my hand as Matron at our town police station, so I knew I could be an assertive security officer. Besides, my patrolling would make the residents feel safer. So I agreed.

On my first night, I was decked out in dark clothing, with a whistle on my wrist. I carried a police flashlight and a cellphone, which was voice activated to directly contact the police station. I loved the job, especially on Bingo nights when I escorted the "Bingo bunnies" back inside from their fun evening event.

I oversaw security for the entire center, both inside and out. One of the tenants had made friends with a stray tomcat, and this tomcat took it upon himself to go on my outside rounds with me. He was my own personal security detail! Thus, he was named "C.O.P.," Cat on Patrol.

Seeking out perpetrators had to be done in stealth, and C.O.P. and I worked in unison, matching calculated step for step, ears alert, breathing low and steady. Three times, I had alerted the police of troublemakers on our property, thanks to C.O.P.

One night, I quickly hid behind a fence when I saw two people approaching. I just knew it was those drunken teenagers again, and C.O.P. and I were going to show them a thing or two this time!

Neither C.O.P. nor I breathed as the two came closer. I crouched down, ready to spring into full security-guard mode, and C.O.P. stood next to me, his ears tilted forward and his tail fluffed up the size of a raccoon's tail. We were ready for a surprise attack!

"Hey, what ya lookin' at?" a voice suddenly said from behind us.

C.O.P. half screamed while leaping 100 feet into the air, and I fell onto my butt, right into a mud puddle! It took me a few seconds to realize that one of the seniors was out for a midnight stroll. With all my focus on the approaching teens, I didn't hear him come up from behind. Of course, with the cat screaming and all the other commotion, the teenagers ran away. All you can do in a situation like this is laugh, which the senior and I did. Due to both the fall on my butt and the unrestrained laughter, I'm glad I had another pair of jeans inside my backpack!

One brisk fall evening soon after that incident, I headed outside for my third lap around the building. It was after midnight, and I had not seen my patrol buddy. *Maybe he's taking the night off*, I thought to myself.

Exiting the front door, I let the double-glass doors swing shut behind me so they would lock. As soon as I was 30 feet from the door, I sensed I was not alone. I hoped to turn around and see that C.O.P. had shown up for duty, but instead, I looked right at Mr. Bear. And he looked back at me!

I didn't stay long. All my bravado flew right out of my head, all the Matron police training was quickly forgotten, my assertiveness melted out through immediate perspiration and thoughts of protecting the seniors to my death were left behind in my skid marks!

I don't even remember the run to the center's south-side

entrance, except that my heart beat in my throat as I franti-cally opened the door. Once inside, I sat down and calmed myself—I assured myself that running had been my only alternative between life and death.

After I regained the use of my legs, I walked to the cof-fee lounge. Removing my coat, I returned to the front door to see if Mr. Bear was gone. But all I saw was C.O.P., sitting outside the door, ready for duty.

"There you are, C.O.P.!" I said to him as I unlocked the door. I wasn't supposed to let him inside, but it was late, and no one would know. Plus, Mr. Bear could still be there unless he had taken off in the other direction after seeing me.

Cool as a cucumber, C.O.P. strolled in. If he had been part of our nightly rounds, his cat senses would have alerted me to the bear's presence. Instead, I had taken away Usain Bolt's title as the world's fastest human.

"C.O.P.! Where were you?" I inquired, like any good cop—ah, security guard—would have done.

The cat looked up at me innocently. He didn't have a care in the world. But looking into his eyes, I saw a glint of humor. I guessed C.O.P. had been hiding in the bushes the entire night because of the bear and was happy I had chased it off with my reaction.

"You coward," I teased C.O.P., giving him a pat on the head. And that's when I saw him smile, mischief dancing in his eyes. The center was safe and Mr. Bear was gone. To C.O.P., it was mission accomplished.

Eddie the Car Cat

by
Janda Rangel

Eddie, our Norwegian Forest cat, is unusual as far as cats go. He's very large, about the size of a 13-pound Pekingese, although he looks like a giant, gray cotton ball.

I've heard many cat owners say that their cherished felines are special, but few are as unique as our Eddie. He was found as a feral kitten and was nurtured by two English Mastiff dogs. The two dogs carried the newborn kitten in their mouths and cared for him as though he were their own.

Eddie was given to us as a young kitten, but "he" was named after a "she"—Esmeralda. At about 10 weeks old, we realized "she" was actually a "he," so we shortened the name to Eddie.

What made Eddie such a different cat was that, as a youngster, he loved riding in cars. On two occasions, friends of my son left our house to drive home, but when they got part way down the road, they found Eddie happily sitting on the passenger seat. Apparently, Eddie hid until the car started moving, and then came out from wherever he was hiding to enjoy the ride.

Eddie was ready to go anywhere at any time. He would even leap into the bed of my husband's truck if he thought he was going somewhere. Once, my husband took a load of Sheetrock, cardboard and other items to the dump, and unbeknownst to us, Eddie had climbed into the bed of the truck, between the layers of debris, and hid.

Once we realized that Eddie had probably become a stowaway on the trip to the dump, we looked everywhere for him, with no luck. After giving up hope, Eddie appeared a week later at our back door. He was thin, his fur was dirty and matted and he whined like a baby. He never told us if he had walked home all the way from the dump, or if he had jumped out of the truck somewhere along the way. Our older dog—that had an amazing bond with Eddie—barked and howled the entire time his friend was missing. We believe it was the dog's howl that guided Eddie home.

From that point, our family learned to keep the car windows rolled up and to check truck beds before pulling away, and we advised visitors to do the same. No telling when Eddie would get the itch to hit the road again.

My son and his wife, Amy, live in a house on our shared property. One afternoon, Amy was having her Ford Explorer fixed by her uncle, who was a mechanic. Working on the car in our driveway, Uncle didn't know about our car-loving cat. With the hood up and the driver's side door open, Eddie jumped into the idling car, undetected. Hiding on the back seat's floorboard, Eddie waited and waited to go for a ride.

Soon after, Amy walked by and casually shut the car door. With the windows rolled up, Eddie climbed into the front seat and looked through the driver's side window to see what was going on. Amy noticed him looking through the window and as she moved toward the door to let him out, the unthinkable happened. With his enormous paw, Eddie pushed down the electronic lock button on the door. It almost seemed intentional. He had locked all four doors. By that time, the entire family was in the driveway, and we were amazed at Eddie's determination to stay in the car.

Amy had one key, which was in the ignition of the now-locked, idling car. Knowing that Eddie was an intelligent cat, she tried to coax him to step on the button again to unlock the doors. He just stared back at her then calmly sauntered over to the passenger seat to take a snooze. Our confident cat knew he had the upper hand and no one was going get him out of that car. We couldn't stop laughing in disbelief. We were convinced Eddie would put the car into drive and cruise away, into the sunset.

Thankfully, Uncle was able to turn the engine off from under the hood. We tried various tricks to unlock the door—an old coat hanger, a Slim Jim—but nothing worked. Using my car, Amy drove to her parent's house to get the extra key. Eddie continued to lounge on the seat, watching us, as if we were there to entertain him.

As the car grew hotter inside, Eddie became tired of his game and blamed us. He glared out the window, watching our every move, irritated we wouldn't open the doors. He complained loudly, meowing as if to ask, "Don't you understand the game is over, I'm hot, and no one is going anywhere?"

After about 45 minutes, Amy returned with the spare key and finally opened the car door. Eddie bolted away—mad at us and the world. I'm sure he was thinking how unfair life was, seeing he didn't get to go for a ride after being so resourceful and clever.

Our unusual cat has instigated many interesting adventures for our family over the years. We can't wait to see what—or where—he'll take us on our next journey. Hopefully he's not the one driving!

Eddie, obviously trying to figure out how to start the car, and Janda

Bustin' a Move

by
Stacey Hatton

Whenever one of my children gets sick, it never fails that I allow them to eat junk food. With that said, however, most of the wicked comfort food makes it into *my* mouth before it nears their sick tray. If I know why I'm doing this, why don't I stop? Let me open up the family-sized box of Cheez-Its and ponder the answer . . .

I seem to be at my worst when I have little control over the situation. The fat, old "Carb Fairy" swirls around my cart at the grocery store, seizing temptations and dropping them into my cart when I'm not focused. Cookies, Doritos, fudge bars, macaroni and cheese—all crapola that rarely makes an appearance in our house.

I'm buying that food to make them feel better?

Who am I kidding?

But I'm here to tell you, that evil nymph broke into to

my house again with a vat of cookie dough ice cream last week, and that sucker didn't stand a chance.

At the beginning of summer 2013, our family adopted two darling kittens from a shelter. My daughters, Munchkin #1 and Munchkin #2, fell instantly in love, but became attached to the one we named "Jazzy." This cat appeared to be more jazzed up the first day when we were naming them, plus her white paws looked like jazz hands. You would never guess I'm a bit of a musical-theater nerd.

The next morning, without any warning, Jazzy decided to perform a double-back flip off our one-story landing onto the bottom stairs of the staircase. Since I was in the next room, I sprinted after hearing a seismic-strength *thud*. There was the two-month-old kitty, weaving into the family room and shaking her head as if a linebacker had just rung her bell.

Unfortunately, Jazzy never was the same after that. Her health declined severely, and she had to leave our home. My daughters—who were age six and seven—were furious and blamed me for the cat's head injury. They said they would never forgive me.

My children can be overly dramatic at times, so I figured I would give it a couple of weeks, and they would warm up to the other cat. Then we could move forward.

One month later . . .

THUD!!

What the heck was that? I wondered. *It sounded just like when Jazzy* . . .

Oh, yes. When this happened to Jazzy, all three of the veterinarians we visited said it was unheard of for a cat to fall off a one-story landing onto the stairs below. SO WHY DID THE SECOND CAT JUST DO IT, TOO?!

Meet Cali, a beautiful calico cat who is quirky and, on a daily basis, likes to mimic breast-feeding on a human's T-shirt. She was odd, but who are we to judge? Our family isn't exactly related to "the Beav" or the Bradys.

But now we had two kittens doing something which is unheard of in feline veterinary medicine. I was thinking that if the shelter got word of this happening, it would assign a caseworker and write me up for a second alleged boot to the puss.

Fast forward to when the urge to start overeating occurred.

"Mrs. Hatton? From Cali's X-rays, it appears she has fractured her hip," said the vet to me over the phone.

As I listened, I grabbed a spoon and headed to the freezer. "She broke her hip? She's just a kitten, not an old lady," I laughed. I tend to make lame jokes when I'm given bad medical news.

The vet continued. "Since it's a clean break at the head of the bone, it looks as if surgery is the only way to save the hip joint."

My head started whirling, my gut began churning and I was craving chocolate awful fierce. I knew that if we didn't save this kitten, life was going to be hell on earth. Or worse— my husband and I would have to sleep with one eye open. Our darling munchkins would lose it!

I know. Who's the parent in this scenario? But sometimes humans—even little ones—can be pushed over the brink and go on crazy parental killing sprees because too many of their beloved kitties were sent off to the "farm."

We weren't willing to sacrifice our lives for a pet. And, if I were gone, who would supply the house with more Cheez-Its?

Plus, I kind of liked Cali. While the munchkins were at school, Cali would climb up on my desk and cuddle near my computer. She would soak up its warmth and keep me company while I tried to write. I called her my writing "mews."

After discussing the surgery in great depth, and deciding the odds of one munchkin getting a college scholarship was a possibility, we were willing to risk the financial setback. I called the vet back and said we would pay the horrifically high amount of . . .

WE INTERRUPT THIS BROADCAST
FOR THE PURPOSE OF DISTRACTION!

This just in: Several veterinary schools in Middle Eastern universities have taken up camel manipulation. Frank, isn't that interesting? Apparently, camels can be injured due to their awkward gait across the unsteady desert terrain. Back to your regular programming.*

So we got Cali's hip fixed, and she began hobbling along much better two days later. The vet said we were to keep her from jumping up on anything for three weeks.

I was sure that would be easy. NOT! But after all the dough we had spent on this kitten, we needed to keep her protected.

Did anybody check Craigslist to see if a "huge hamster ball" is for sale?

Until we have that in place, or have figured how to make a cat suit of Bubble Wrap, I'm going to be holding my breath and making frequent trips for more ice cream.

*No facts were checked by this author on camel manipulations. It sounds way too gross.

Jazzy resting in-between her dance numbers

The Kid in the Orange Fur Suit

by

Tina Wagner-Mattern

When our cat, Brodie, was born, his mother developed a breast infection. For this reason, he and his siblings had to be nurtured and hand-fed by their human grandmother, my good friend Ellen.

Ellen tended them devotedly. Hers was the first face the kittens saw in the morning and the last one at night. In their minds, Ellen was their mom, and since she was human, they must have been, too. Consequently, Brodie had no idea he was a cat—as far as he was concerned, he was a vertically challenged kid in an orange fur suit.

From the first day that Brodie came to live with us, we could see that he, like his surrogate mom, was a people-person. His philosophy was clear: "Strangers are just friends you haven't met yet." He was crazy about everybody. And he was certain that everyone felt the same way about him. Whenever the doorbell rang, Brodie would jump up and bolt for the door, radiating excitement as if to say, "Someone's here to visit me!" Salesmen, visiting friends or family were welcomed with Brodie's hyperdrive purring and head-butting enthusiasm.

One afternoon, we had a repairman in our home to fix our refrigerator. Brodie was ecstatic to meet him and followed him like a puppy to the kitchen. I was busying myself around the house with laundry and dusting when I heard a deep male laugh coming from behind the fridge. I peeked around the corner to find the man down on his hands and knees, working. Brodie was perched on his shoulder, supervising.

"Good grief," I groaned. "Brodie, get down!"

The man laughed again and said, "Nah, it's OK. He's just helping."

Brodie flashed me a smug look and made himself useful by giving the nice man a shoulder massage.

Throughout the years Brodie was with us, our furry little goodwill ambassador took great pride in his charismatic charm. Even those folks who were "not cat people" somehow changed their minds when confronted with Brodie's sweet, seductive attention. He reigned undefeated until the day our beautiful friend, Terra, came to stay with us for a month.

Terra loves animals—all animals—cats included. But she is very allergic to the fur of felines. One touch and she breaks out in hives, her sinuses go nuts and she's just generally miserable. So it's understandable that she would avoid like the plague being in close proximity to a cat.

Brodie took one look at Terra when she walked in the door and fell head-over-paws in love. Our dear friend apparently exuded some mysterious human-catnip essence that Brodie found absolutely irresistible. Food, toys, even coveted kitty treats were suddenly unimportant to Brodie—getting close to Terra became his prime directive.

With no doubt as to his reception, Brodie waited until his beloved sat down on the sofa, and then he launched himself into her lap. Placing his paws on her chest, he turned on his purr-box full-throttle and stared meaningfully into Terra's eyes. This gambit had always guaranteed quality petting in the past. Terra giggled, all the while trying to push Brodie away without actually touching him with her hands.

"Brodie!" I cried, "Get down!" When he completely ignored me, I retrieved him and sat him down beside me. "You can't bother Terra," I explained. "She's allergic to you."

Apparently, Brodie wasn't buying it. As soon as our attention was diverted by conversation, he was right back in Terra's lap again. Variations of this scene continued to be played throughout the next month. Brodie pursued Terra as single-mindedly as a starving ant at a Martha Stewart picnic.

One evening, after Terra headed upstairs to get ready for bed, I heard her laugh aloud. "Tina—you've got to see this!" she called.

I ran upstairs and found her in the bathroom, where Brodie—wearing an expression of triumph—was on his back in her sink. The message was clear: "If you want me out of here, you gotta pick me up!" I did just that, to Brodie's chagrin. Terra kept the bathroom door closed from then on.

After that episode, I could almost see the wheels turning in Brodie's little head. There would be no more pussyfooting around, as our determined little fur ball was not to be defeated so easily.

A few evenings later, after Terra was settled in for the night, I was once again summoned by a squeal and giggle. Brodie had flown into her room, pounced onto her bed, and had begun massaging her back.

"Guess you're going to have to keep the bedroom door closed, too," I sighed.

I picked Brodie up and took him with me downstairs. "Now listen," I told him, in no uncertain terms, "You have to leave Terra alone! She's ALLERGIC!" Brodie sulked for the rest of the evening, but somewhere in his creative little head, a new plan was already hatching.

It took several days to work out the logistics, but once Brodie figured his new strategy was foolproof, he settled down to wait patiently for the perfect time. It didn't take long.

I had watched a movie with Terra and my husband, Fred, and we were pleasantly surprised that throughout the evening, Brodie hadn't even attempted any of his usual ploys for his sweetheart's attention. In fact, he seemed to have mysteriously disappeared.

"Maybe he's finally losing interest," I said, hopefully.

Terra just smiled, "He's so sweet, poor little guy. Well, I'm off to bed."

Upstairs, Terra put on her pajamas, washed her face and brushed her teeth, all the while keeping an eye out for her little stalker. But Brodie was still nowhere to be seen. "Goodnight!" she called out to us, and, taking one last look around for her furry shadow, opened her bedroom door and went in, closing it behind her. Once in bed, she sighed contentedly, turned off the light and settled herself for a good night's sleep.

She was just dozing off when . . . *foomph!* An 8-pound kid in an orange fur suit landed squarely on her chest, purring jubilantly. His strategy had worked! Hiding under the bed for two hours had paid off. Surely, his sweetheart would finally see that they were meant to be together!

We could hear Terra's laughter and wheezing all the way downstairs. Her amended nightly routine from then on included checking for furry little monsters under the bed.

Brodie was one of the dearest members of our family for many years. He was unfailingly sweet, clever and irresistible. We have countless memories of him to treasure, but none as unforgettable as the time our boy set out to win Terra's heart.

Brodie

Here's Kitty!

by
Robley J. Barnes

Late on a December Friday night, my wife awakened me with the news that she had heard strange sounds in the attic. I assured her it was only birds or squirrels on the roof and went back to sleep.

Saturday night, and again Sunday night, those strange sounds became more prominent. *Thump. . . scratch . . . MEOW!* There was a cat in our attic!

On Monday, I climbed into the attic to meet the critter face-to-furry face. My call of, "Here kitty, kitty," was met with a frightened stare from the animal, which was sitting at an inaccessible part of the attic near an eave.

Visits to the neighbors yielded a bamboo pole and some lightweight rope—and laughter about the situation. It was to have been a simple matter to capture that feline using this pole-loop device. However, upon entry into the attic, no cat was seen or heard.

"Maybe it got out the same way it got in," a neighbor offered. That was my hope, because I didn't want anything to happen to the cat.

Note of explanation: Our home had a carport with a utility/storage room at one end. It housed a washer and dryer and also a water heater, which vented through a large opening in the ceiling. On the aforementioned Friday, a cat had apparently entered the utility room, jumped onto the washer, and then onto the water heater, and finally into the attic.

Tuesday night, we heard the same sounds. This cat was playing games with us—and winning. Calls to the humane shelter and the fire department received sympathy, but no action. Neither did a call to a pest-control company.

The next day, we had to leave town to visit family. Fearful that "Kitty" would starve during our absence, I placed bits of ham and bowls of milk in the attic.

While visiting my parents, my dad and I constructed a humane animal trap, using scraps of plywood, Masonite, wire and string. On returning home four days later, all the ham and milk had been consumed and an occasional *meow* could still be heard. The attic trap was baited and set and some ham was laid out on the washer, as well. I even opened the utility room door, hoping Kitty would escape to freedom.

The next morning, the trap bait was gone, and so was the chunk of ham that had been on the washer. This little critter was having a ball tantalizing me, and was probably gaining weight in the process.

New strategy! The trap was moved to the utility/store

room for easier access by the "dummy human"—that's me—and hopefully to lure Kitty further down from the hole.

The next morning, the trap door was closed. Eureka! Success at last. Not! The crisscrossed wire at the end of the trap had been manipulated in such a way that a very small hole had been made. Kitty had gotten its body through the hole—which I estimate was about one-third of its body size—and had returned to its home in the attic.

With the trap revised and reinforced, I devised a manually operated door release by using some fishing line. The plan was to wait for Kitty at the kitchen door, where the utility/storage door was easily visible. When Kitty appeared, I would pull the line to close the trap door. Again, I made sure the utility room door was open in case Kitty wanted to flee from the house instead.

I watched and waited for a short time, when suddenly, "Here's Kitty." It had won again. I had accidentally left some extra ham wrapped in foil on the washer. Ignoring the meat in the trap, Kitty took the entire package back to the attic.

About an hour later, my nemesis had returned. This time, Kitty entered the trap, but only halfway—the door couldn't drop all the way, because the cat blocked it. Kitty backed out slowly, and then turned to look outside through the open door. But Kitty chose not to take advantage of potential freedom—the cat knew it had a good thing going.

Since it was late in the evening, the automatic trap-door release was again set and I went to bed.

Finally, the next morning, the cat had been securely caught. During those 12 days and nights, that furry critter consumed 6 quarts of whole milk and 4 pounds of smoked ham.

We released Kitty in the front yard in hopes it would find its rightful home. The cat immediately ran about 30 feet away, stopped, looked back at me and meowed twice. Then it disappeared into the neighborhood. I think Kitty's meows were its way of saying, "Thanks for the good food and hospitality." Cats really do rule their world!

The Pen Gremlin

by

Jordan Bernal

Have you ever agreed to pet sit for a friend? I did once. It sounded like the perfect gig. I'm a writer and what better way to get some quiet writing time than away from the daily chores and interruptions of my life? I packed up my writing instruments—computer, manuscript, notes and a favorite pen—to spend a week in someone else's space with one dog and two cats.

I have my own pet, a two-year-old dog. Not being a cat owner, I assumed the two cats would be less time-consuming and less hassle than the dog. Wrong!

Sonja, a black and orange cat whom I nicknamed "Runaway" for her penchant to escape when humans turned their backs, made good on her moniker the night before I was to drive her human to the airport. She had escaped—again.

Scouring the block, we called out for Sonja. Armed with the flashlight application on my iPhone, I spotted her across the street and around the corner from the house. She wouldn't come to me, so I hurried back to get her owner. The two of us continued the search, whispering instead of yelling for the well-hidden recalcitrant one since it was past 11 P.M. and we didn't want the neighbors calling 911.

Around midnight, we gave up and headed to bed since we needed to leave early for the airport the next morning. At 5:30 A.M., we found Runaway—she graced us with her presence by the garage door. I had survived the first pet incident.

Now on my own with my new pets, the days were quiet. To my surprise, Runaway and Izzy—the other cat—were mellow. Translation—they were comatose nappers. But not so after I retired. As soon as I laid my head on the pillow, I heard cat paws scurrying down the hardwood-floor hallway. Toys, empty food and water dishes, pots and pans and who knew what else crashed and banged. It sounded like they were having a party with 10 cat friends who had snuck in to join the nighttime mayhem. Several nights in a row, I'd rise to check the house for intruders. No one was around, nothing was out of place. The cats' antics didn't seem to bother Gretchen, the dog, who slept soundly in her crate each night.

As a writer, I have my idiosyncrasies, habits, superstitions. Similar to an athlete wearing the same socks or eating the same meal before each game, I always write the bare bones of a scene in longhand. Then I flesh out the complete scene as I dictate into my computer, using voice-recognition software.

Like the athlete, I rely on a good luck charm—my special pen. This one pen has my manuscript in it. Other writing implements exist, but none has my story flowing from its tip. When the ink runs dry, I buy replacement ink tubes. The pen itself holds my story. Crazy, I know, but superstitions are strong, magical forces.

One evening, I left my work open on the dining room table, with my pen resting on the written pages. Sometime after midnight, Runaway and Izzy began their nocturnal, raucous shenanigans. Once again, I checked for human intruders, found none and headed back to bed.

Morning dawned and I emerged to find a thief had indeed been in the house during the night. My laptop sat in the open where I'd left it. The TV, stereo and other electronics were still in their places. The only missing item was my pen. My magical, manuscript-infused writing instrument. The pen that molds to my fingers, the pen that warms to my touch, the pen that flows across the page as my story flows through its silver body.

I narrowed my eyes at the two felines, whose expressions said, "Who, us?" They gave no hint as to where my pen had disappeared. I searched everywhere. I peered under couches, crouched under the dining room table and chairs, pulled cushions and throw pillows from couches and beds. I whipped the drapes away from the potted plants.

Where could my beloved pen be?! I wondered, in a panic. The house had been locked up tight, but I ran outside anyway. I scoured the backyard, the garage. My pen was nowhere. I repeated my room-by-room search, eight in all. Gone. *What to do?* My story was in that pen. The last four years of my life were in that pen. Another just wouldn't do.

I shuffled to the dining room table, dejected. I pulled

out a chair to sit and mourn. My bare foot landed on a bump under the throw rug beneath the table. I whipped back the edge of the black-and-white patterned rug.

Eureka! My beloved pen, my story!

I turned, eyeing the suspected thieves. Runaway lay sprawled asleep on the back of the couch. Izzy, however, meandered over to me with a mischievous gleam in her eyes. She swiped at my pen.

I clasped it tighter. "Mine," I told her. I gazed at the disturbed furnishings and shook my head as the sassy cat tried for my pen again. "Not on your nine lives."

Later, I'd investigate a safe hiding place for my pen, a place that even the Pen Gremlin would not be able to find. So much for my quiet, hassle-free writing time. Wish me luck.

Izzy, Jordan and the pen

Kung-Fu Cat

by
Dena Harris

My husband and I enjoy a soothing morning ritual of relaxing with the fish. We sit together on the couch in semi-darkness, sipping coffee and watching the fish dive and swerve through the water in the fish tank. Sometimes we talk, sometimes we don't. It's a peaceful opening to the day before the world intrudes.

Of course, if you have cats, the world always intrudes, usually in a harsh and abrasive manner. For example, the other morning as we sat quietly, contemplating the fish, suddenly Kung-Fu Cat appeared and attacked the tank.

"WAH-HAH-HEE-AIIIEEEE-YAH!" The cat dashed in from the hall, leapt onto the dining room chair we keep in front of the fish tank for kitty-viewing pleasure, and began pummeling the glass barrier. Her four paws were a blur of high leg kicks and karate chops. Maybe it was just the way her tail was hanging, but I swear she was sporting a black belt.

Fish scattered, my husband and I jolted upright and Kung-Fu Cat—having made her point—bowed to the fish, leapt off the chair and raced from the room.

"Is she high?" my husband asked, brushing spilled coffee from his robe.

I have no idea what gets into her. After 80-billion attempts—including a memorable hang-gliding incident—one would think she would have clued in by now that the fish tank is impenetrable. But no. Apparently, she's now invested in ancient Eastern martial arts as holding the key to sushi success.

What concerns me most is that Kung-Fu Cat appears to have taken on our other cat—a kitten—as her padawan learner. This doesn't bode well. Any situation that sets up the cat as master of anything is a mistake in my book.

They sit together in the hall, the kitten bowing low before the cat. Actually, the kitten wasn't so much bowing as it was the cat was sitting on her. The cat shifted slightly and placed a gentle paw on the kitten's head. "Ah, grasshopper. The way of the humble is the first step toward inner mastery. And so . . . uh, I command you to always grovel before me," Kung-Fu Cat paused, looking thoughtful, "and to give me all your food."

"Stop," I said to the cat. "This is rubbish."

She gave me a dirty look.

"Glare all you want," I said. "But I'm watching the kitten eat to make sure she gets her fill. And, by the way, go put my hooded sweatshirt back in the closet. Wearing it makes you look nothing like a Jedi-master."

The next morning, my husband and I sat near the fish and tried again. All appeared tranquil. For the time being, anyway. But I doubted it would remain so. Yesterday, I caught the kitten online, attempting to secure home delivery of a light-saber she found on eBay. I think she has visions of slicing through the walls of the fish tank, only to stand over a small, gasping goldfish and announce, "I AM YOUR FATHER."

Kung-Fu Cat is worse. We hear her day and night, out in the hall, huffing and puffing as she goes through her exercise routine.

Someone had better warn the fish—or at least teach them the rudimentary ways of the Force or the Dark Side. Because that cat is getting good with those high kicks.

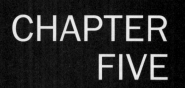

The Joy
of Cats

Feline fancy at its finest.

Holy Cats!

by
John Evangelist Schlimm II

For several years, I got to enjoy watching, and even partaking in, a daily routine that took place Monday through Saturday at St. Joseph Monastery in St. Marys, Pennsylvania, out of view of most visitors.

Early in the morning, as the sun climbed over the oldest Benedictine convent in the United States, two cats would awaken from their various perches inside the ceramic shop. One, a calico, was named Blitzen and the other was named Tommy, because he was a striking black-and-white tomcat. It's not quite certain where they slept from night to night, but it was suspected that they nuzzled cozily in between the decades-old ceramic molds stacked on shelves in the back room, and, occasionally, on the highest shelf in the kiln room where, just below, fragile greenware pieces stood ready to be fired.

Once awake, the cats sauntered out into the front room, where shelves filled with statues of Jesus and Mary and the occasional saint, vases, ornaments, bowls, piggy banks, crucifixes, and even decanters shaped like Napoleon and Santa Claus, awaited shoppers. The two cats, each with a St. Francis medal around his neck, were waiting for someone very special to arrive.

After mass and breakfast, 91-year-old Sr. M. Augustine, O.S.B., would make her way out of the convent's main building and, with the help of her cane, down the cement steps to an attached building called the Guesthouse that was home to her ceramic shop. On her way, she'd survey her nearby flower gardens and perhaps pause a moment to listen to a set of wind chimes, a gift I and two other friends had given to her, welcoming the morning with their unique jingling outside her shop door.

Once inside, Sister was warmly greeted by Blitzen and Tommy, who danced around, nipping at her long, traditional black robe. Then sometimes they'd dash off hurriedly, tempting Sister into a game of hide and seek, which would last all day.

Starting in 1964, Sr. Augustine literally painted her way across the country and the globe with a long lineage of friendly felines always at her side. There's at least one of her hand-painted Nativity sets in every state in the U.S., and her small crosses made from leftover clay and other items have landed in such faraway places as Central America, Europe, Africa, Asia and Russia.

Each day, as Sister poured wet clay into molds, cleaned the rough edges of the greenware, or sat painting her most popular item, the *Gussie's Special*—bowls and vases covered with leftover glaze that emerged from the kiln as divine masterpieces—Blitzen and Tommy were always nearby. They never failed to induce a twinkle in Sister's signature smile.

Sr. Augustine often took breaks to play with the cats, though usually out of view of customers. She would tease Blitzen with a homemade toy, consisting of an artificial daisy attached to a string. Slowly Sister would bait the calico, resting the daisy on the floor and holding the string. As the cat approached, Sister, with a tug and a chuckle, would make the daisy bounce and Blitzen pounce. About this time, Tommy would make his way through, batting a tiny stuffed mouse with his paw. However, the minute the front door opened and I walked in, he always fled into the back room.

I would visit Sister at least once or twice a week. Over the years, Blitzen and Tommy warmed to me. Blitzen and I even touched nose to nose once, Eskimo-style. "You're lucky," Sister told me, "Blitzen doesn't normally like guys." Tommy was always in too much of a hurry to pay attention to me after I settled in for a chat.

"Blitzen likes to drink the water I rinse my brushes in, so I have to cover it now," Sister told me one afternoon, pointing to the sealed container filled with murky water. "And he loves the rain! Have you ever heard of a cat who likes to get wet?"

Sister's face then registered disapproval followed by sheer elation as her furry co-worker leapt up onto the table, gliding precariously through the maze of open paint bottles and clayware. "You know you're not allowed up there!" Sister admonished gently. Sometimes Blitzen listened and sometimes he enjoyed the liberty of ignoring his personal mother superior.

"It's that time," Sister said a few minutes later, after Blitzen had once more hopped off the table. "Time for Blitzen's nap." She then directed my attention to her feet, beneath the table.

I bent down to see Blitzen rubbing up against Sister's robed leg.

"Come on up," Sister spoke sweetly to him, while patting her lap.

Blitzen jumped up and immediately settled in. Sister gently brushed Blitzen's shiny gold-and-white coat. "You like it up here, don't you?" she cooed. "Have you seen Tommy yet?" she then asked me.

"Not really," I replied. I had only seen flashes of black and white once, darting in through one doorway, under the table, swatting a few boxes along the way, and out another door.

When I would be there for a morning visit, I knew Sister had to leave for prayers and lunch by 11:45 A.M., so I would bid her farewell until the next week. When Sister left for lunch, the front window was always left open a crack, just enough so Blitzen and Tommy could come and go as they pleased. What I wouldn't have given to be with them as they traversed the vast and historic convent grounds—more than 150 years old, frolicking and occasionally, to Sr. Augustine's chagrin, nabbing a bird.

When Sister returned from lunch, some afternoons were slow, allowing Blitzen to once more cuddle on her lap as she painted. Both might then steal a short nap, Sister would tell me, while Tommy was still busy out on the grounds or perhaps resting lazily on one of the walkways heated by the sun.

As the clock neared five each afternoon, Sister would clean up for the day and bid Blitzen and Tommy good night. The shop was where they'd stay, for it was their home—a cat's fantasy playground if ever there was one. Sister then gathered her cane and trekked back up the outside steps and into the convent for afternoon prayers and supper. The cats watched her go from the windowsill.

No one ever really knew what happened after that, but Sister and I had fun, and many, many laughs, imagining the adventures Blitzen and Tommy must have had in the dark, racing around after one another and sneaking up and over the full shelves, only rarely leaving a shattered trail behind them as evidence of their dalliances.

What is for sure is in the morning they'd once more be waiting at the front door to welcome Sister back.

Sr. Augustine and Blitzen

Stella's Conquest

by
Cheryl Anne Stapp

It was late summer, the time of soft winds from the Sacramento Delta and promised glorious sunsets, the time when my husband and I usually spent after-dinner evenings relaxing on our back porch.

Neighborhood cats regularly patrolled our wooden fence spines, sometimes lithely dropping down into the yard for a sniff at this or that. They would occasionally favor me with a quick glance before leaping away to other adventures. But one evening, we had a surprise. We heard a loud, repeated, insistent *MEEEOOOWWW* coming from the direction of our add-on covered patio.

"Kitty?" I said, hoping to locate the voice's source.

Suddenly, a little black-and-white cat dashed out from under the raised-beam flooring where she had been hiding, coming straight toward me without, apparently, a single care for her safety. She continued to communicate, but in gentler tones: "HereIamhereIamhereIam!" Maybe she already knew, from covert reconnaissance, that we sheltered two adult cats inside the house, or maybe she had spied on me from her hiding place often enough to feel that I might be receptive to feline damsels in distress.

She looked like a young animal, maybe six months to less than a year old. She was a pretty little thing, with medium-long hair and big, dark-gold eyes. Her attire was more feminine than a formal tuxedo coat. She had white cheeks, shoulders, front paws and tummy. From behind, she looked completely black, except for a thin white necklace of fur around her collarbone.

When she sat down near my sandaled feet and looked up politely, I asked her several questions. What was her name? Where did she live? Who might be missing her? Was she hungry?

There was no answer as she sniffed my outstretched fingers. *Water*, I thought. *She needs water. I'll fill the empty flower bowl on the porch table.*

Unfortunately, when I stood up and reached for the hose, she bolted, in a leaping, bounding movement that struck me as more deer-like than cat-like.

She came back the next day and every evening thereafter for 10 days, always at the same time, 7:30. Her comings and goings were mysterious—I never knew which side of our fenced yard she crawled over, or where she disappeared to after darkness. She ignored the little bowl of cat kibble I had offered. *Does she have a home where someone feeds her then lets her outside to roam?* That wasn't a good idea, in my opinion.

Our neighborhood backs up against open fields where coyotes are occasionally seen. Still, she didn't look or act starved.

My husband mentioned that he had seen a black-and-white cat killing birds in the vacant yard next door. *Could she be this huntress?* Cats hunt prey even when they're getting meals from loving humans, so that alone told me nothing.

It was obvious, though, that she was, or had been, someone's pet. She always sat near my feet, her big gold eyes fixed on my face, listening attentively while I talked to her. She accepted my stroking and allowed me to pick her up to sit on my knees, where she curled up and purred. On the fourth night, I caught her gazing wistfully at me through the glass sliding door after I went inside.

She was very calm and quite friendly during our little chats, unless another neighborhood cat temporarily entered the yard—and then, oh, my! Such rumbling, rising and falling growls emanated from her tiny throat, even when the interloper was 40 feet away. It was a bluff, of course, because she stayed close to my chair instead of dashing across the grass to engage the other in combat.

About the seventh day of her visits, I began to notice that her white fur looked increasingly dirty, too dirty for a cat that spent any extended time indoors, and I convinced myself that she had probably been abandoned. The housing market in California then was in a state of free-fall and "for sale" signs were appearing here and there on every block. As any animal shelter employee knows, all too often pets are left behind on their own when families are forced to move elsewhere.

This thought presented a dilemma. The environment was too dangerous for a domesticated pet to successfully fend for herself for anything close to a cat's mythical nine lifetimes. But we already had two cats, both smugly sure of their place in the household and each other. They weren't likely to accept a rival in their midst. An animal shelter was one logical answer. She would be safe from predators there, but we worried about how long. Hundreds of would-be adoptees don't find new owners. The thought of her being put down when her allotted time at the shelter was up made me shudder. I didn't want her to stay outside in the cruel world, either. *Maybe I can find her a family.*

On the 11th day, we brought her inside and closed her in a bedroom where she was safe and snug with her own food and litter box. The next evening, I knocked on every door on the street, asking if anyone had lost a pretty little black-and-white cat. No one had. One woman three doors down was sympathetic, but had no idea to whom she might belong. Next, I posted flyers at every cluster mailbox within five blocks. No response.

Meanwhile, the little sequestered beauty ramped up her efforts to win our hearts. Each time we entered her sanctuary, she offered joyous greetings, contented purrs and soft ankle rubs. Her gentle eye-blinks said, "I choose you. Won't you choose me too?" What a seductress! I couldn't just keep calling her "Kitty," could I? She needed a proper name. From several choices, she seemed to like "Stella" best.

One evening when I was in the front yard, the friendly neighbor lady stopped her car and rolled down her window.

She asked if I had found that cat's owner yet.

"No," I said, "not yet. But I named her, just until someone shows up."

"Well," said the grinning lady, "if no one else has claimed her and you've given her a name, it looks like you have yourself a new cat."

We took Stella to the veterinarian to be sure she had no diseases that could infect our other pets. To our surprise, the vet estimated her age at close to five years. She weighed in at a healthy 7 pounds and had a tiny, almost faded spay scar, but no identification chip.

Once home, it was time to introduce Stella to her feline brother and sister. Instant war ensued. Hisses, spits, spats and yowls tore from all three throats, accompanied by attempted paw-slaps from queen bee Annie. But the loudest angry warnings were Stella's. She immediately commandeered our bedroom—not a friendly move. The bedroom wasn't Annie's particular domain, but 20-pound Frazier had a penchant for sleeping on the end of the bed. Little Stella chased him off, repeatedly, until he was too cowed to try again.

Over time—a long time, actually—tempers cooled, but an uneasy truce still prevails. Stella has accepted Frazier as a sometimes napping partner but stays clear of Annie. Annie, for her part, throws Stella the evil eye at every opportunity. Each kitty has its own way of expressing affection to us. Annie is an inveterate lap sitter. Frazier likes face rubs. Stella's preference, in addition to cuddling close at night, is to leap on the back of my upholstered armchair and lick my hair.

Stella, the little one who inveigled her way into our home,

remains vigilant. On summer nights, Stella sits behind the screen door, growling, "Goawaygoawaygoaway," to every curious feline who dares to cross the back porch, lest they try to appropriate the booty that is hers by right of conquest.

Stella

Take My Breath Away

by

Pamela Wright

"He looks like Barbra Streisand," my mother said. "That's what you should call him."

"He" was my newly adopted five-month-old kitten. He had huge, closely set golden eyes that were ever-so-slightly crossed. My mother was not entirely wrong—there was a strong resemblance. It was a little disturbing.

The animal shelter had described the kitten as a Russian Blue mix. His downy fur was indeed a soft blue-gray. But the body composition was pure Siamese—long and lanky with a triangular face framed by large ears. He had the longest tail I'd ever seen on any cat that wasn't hunting sloths in the rainforest.

The kitten cried a bit on the ride home, but once he was released from the confines of the carrier, he explored his new home with a confident curiosity before turning his attention to his newly acquired human. I sat cross-legged on the floor and the kitten scrambled onto my lap. He raised himself straight up on his back legs, the long tail serving as ballast, and slowly stretched a paw toward my cheek. I leaned my face closer to him and he began to sniff intently around my mouth. I had once read that big cats such as lions and tigers acquaint themselves by mutual breath sniffing. In my opinion, this was a far more dignified means of introduction than that done by their canine counterparts.

I had never seen a housecat do this. I held my breath for as long as I could while the kitten continued sniffing, around and around my mouth in tight clockwise circles. I began to wonder if there was something about this kitty that the shelter had failed to disclose. Fearing that I might soon faint, I finally exhaled. The kitten took one long, last sniff and then closed his eyes and began to purr. I felt my cheeks redden. I wasn't sure if I had passed some sort of inspection or just had really bad breath.

We would repeat this ritual every day of his life.

Within a few days of his arrival, I christened the kitten "Harper," in homage to Ms. Harper Lee, the author of my favorite book, *To Kill a Mockingbird.*

"But isn't your kitten a boy?" was the inevitable question from those who made the literary connection.

This point of anatomical clarification was of little consequence to me. A Georgian since birth and a book nerd since the age of four, I had a long tradition of naming pets after Southern writers and their characters. Besides, the kitten didn't know he was named after a woman. And if he did, I was quite confident he would much prefer to be called Harper Lee than Barbra Streisand.

Harper matured into a lively and unflaggingly friendly cat, but the list of his eccentricities lengthened with each passing year. He refused all offers of tuna or salmon, but loved yellow mustard and vegan pepperoni. I once made the mistake of attempting to eat both in his presence simultaneously. It did not end well. My sweet little kitty leapt into the middle of my plate and growled at me as if I were an interloping Rottweiler. It was one of those low, menacing grumbles that emanate from deep in the throat of a seriously pissed-off feline. I call this the "back-off-or bleed, bitch!" warning shot. Before I could defend my dinner, he snatched the sandwich in his mouth and dragged it from the room.

I never did get all of the mustard stains out of that rug.

This would prove to be one of several food-related peculiarities. Left to his own devices, Harper would have gladly snacked on toothpaste. If I should happen to splatter a bit of Crest on my nightclothes during my bedtime toilette, he would graciously remove it during the night, together with a bit of fabric for good measure. I sometimes woke to find small, damp holes had been chewed in my pajama top as I slept.

I went to great efforts to insure that Harper always had a high-quality diet. Among other more traditional reasons, I needed to make up for his occasional indulgences in dentifrice and vegetarian deli food. He was generally an enthusiastic eater, but, on occasion, he would take issue with his evening tin of human-grade, organically farmed, grossly overpriced cat food. After a bite or two, Harper would stop chewing and begin to rake at the floor surrounding his plate. Right paw, left paw, right paw, left paw, again and again, over and over. It looked exactly as if he were covering a fresh deposit in his litter box. I admit I took a bit of offense to this behavior. While I certainly didn't expect him to eat anything he didn't like, at nearly $3 per tiny can, I could have done without the commentary.

Harper's quirky behavior was not limited to food. For a

time, he loved to play in water and could splash a toilet completely dry in three minutes flat. This pastime was eventually abandoned upon his apparent discovery that the antique rocking chair in my bedroom was possessed by demons, which could only be kept at bay by vicious daily attacks.

Having vanquished all evil forces from the house, Harper then designated himself Chief Executive in Charge of Shoe Maintenance and spent long hours in the bottom of the closet, polishing my many pairs of high-heeled sling backs with his tongue. But regardless of whatever other activity captured his imagination from time to time, his primary pursuit in life remained his self-appointed role as four-legged Breathalyzer.

Every human being who crossed Harper's path, friend or family, salesman or deliveryman, was subject to random inspection. Most were utterly charmed by this breath-smelling behavior. Whereas many cats are perceived as aloof and arrogant, Harper was blessed with an endearing absence of pride. Others, however, found his method of introduction downright discomfiting.

Over the years, I became so accustomed to the ritualized breath sniffing that I often forgot to warn people about it. I would sometimes leave a newly arrived houseguest seated on the living room sofa while I prepared drinks or checked on dinner, only to return to find Harper dead center in the lap of an utterly-bewildered human. His pose was always exactly the same—raised straight up on his back legs, with one front paw stretched to the cheek and his nose planted squarely against his quarry's mouth.

Harper: "Sniff. Sniff. Sniff, sniff, sniff."

Human: "G-g-good kitty. N-n-nice kitty."

Harper: "Sniffsniffsniffsniffsniffsniff."

Human: "What's he doing? What the hell is he DO-ING?"

I had every expectation of spending the next decade or so cataloging Harper's eccentricities, the mostly enchanting but sometimes exasperating qualities that I had grown to love in equal measure. But this was not to be. In the spring of his eighth year, Harper developed a malignancy that ravaged his tiny body as quickly as wildfire.

We spent our last moments together exactly as we had our first. Harper stretched one front paw to reach my cheek. I leaned my face in close to his as he struggled to raise his head from the steel examination table. He pressed his nose to the corner of my mouth, as gently as an angel's kiss.

Harper

A Purr-fect Pardon

by
Pat Nelson

"Can you believe the lady down the street is trapping cats?" I asked my next-door neighbor.

"What do you mean?" she asked.

"Yesterday, she stopped by and asked me for a description of my cat and wrote it down on a yellow legal pad like she thinks she's captain of the Cat Police. Said she was headed straight to the pound to get a trap and warned me to keep my cat off her property."

"I don't think you have anything to worry about. Who would drive an hour and a half round trip just to pick up a pet trap?" my neighbor replied.

"She'd better not trap my Hobo. Maybe she doesn't like his loud meow, but that poor old boy . . . he's so deaf he can't hear his own voice anymore."

A few days later, while I soaked in a hot tub, I heard my neighbor frantically telling my answering machine, "She's trapped a cat, and it's a big black-and-white tuxedo. Looks like Hobo. If no one claims him in half an hour, she's taking him to the pound. You're not answering, and I don't know what to do."

We'll see about that, I thought, as I quickly ran a towel over my body and slid some jeans over my damp legs. I finished dressing and headed out the door and down the street, where I found the cat hater standing proudly next to a cage containing a big tuxedo cat. The cat's fur was standing out like porcupine quills, and his eyes were wide with fear.

"Hobo, are you all right, buddy?" I asked.

"Your cat?" she asked, visibly disappointed to have been caught in the act of trapping my pet.

"Looks like him," I said, "but the poor thing's so scared, it's hard to tell for sure."

I bent down to open the cage, and her worn leather boot firmly planted itself in front of the wire door.

"Don't let him out unless you're sure he's yours!" she said, her face contorted with anger. "I'm plenty tired of all these nasty felines doing their business in my rose garden and howling under my bedroom window."

I realized that if I wanted to save Hobo from this vicious woman, I'd have to act quickly and take him to the safety of my home. I grabbed the handle of the cage and hurried toward my house. The cat shifted inside the cage, making the lopsided load difficult to carry.

I walked as fast as I could, but the trapper—not burdened by a heavy crate—easily matched my pace.

"You sure it's *your* cat?" she asked, raising her left eyebrow and striking an almighty pose. "If it's not, he's going to the pound. This damned cat yowls so I can hear him for a block. Like I told you, I want to be sure he's yours before I release him."

"Oh, he's mine, all right. And you've scared six of his nine lives right out of him."

I reached the door of my house, flung it open and released the door of the cage. The cat saw his opportunity to escape. He raced from the cage to the spare bedroom. I handed the trapper the empty cage and slammed the door shut between us.

The cat was free, but it would take time for him to recover from the trauma. I lay on my tile floor, peering under the bed through dust bunnies and plastic army men left by the grandchildren, staring into pure fear.

"Come out, Hobo," I said, but he wouldn't budge. I slowly reached my hand toward him, but brought it back quickly to reveal a long, bloody scratch.

"Poor boy," I said. "You're so scared. You've never scratched me before. I'll just leave you alone and let you calm down."

I set his food and water bowl near the bed and added a bribe of canned tuna to entice him out of his hiding place. I left the room, softly shutting the door behind me, and called my husband to give him a full report.

When he came home from work, he went into the room and called loudly to Hobo. There was no response. He looked under the bed. Hobo was not there. He searched the closet, looked between teddy bears and building blocks, and still couldn't find him. The cat had vanished from a closed room!

We gave up and went out to dinner. Upon our return, my husband opened the bedroom door and searched again for our old friend. That's when a faint plea for help came from the bed. It didn't sound like Hobo's usual loud bellow. Still, we couldn't find him.

We pulled off the bedspread and the pillows. No Hobo. We pulled off the sheets. No Hobo. Finally, as a last resort, we removed the mattress. There he was, between the mattress and the box springs, looking like a cartoon character that had been flattened by a steamroller.

I left the room while my husband firmly held our terrified cat, petted his shiny black coat and repeated calming words.

Movement outside the living room glass door caught my attention. There, begging with loud meows, was our Hobo.

What? Then whose cat is that in the bedroom? I said to myself. I shared the news with my husband that the Hobo he was holding wasn't *our* Hobo.

Learning of this discovery, my husband opened the bedroom's private bath, which had a door to the outside that he also opened, allowing the mystery cat a chance to escape and return home. But the next morning, he was still in there. Then we left the bedroom window open, as well, and waited. We checked again, but fear had glued him to the spot.

In the afternoon, I went to town. When I returned, a neighbor who lived a block away was walking away from my house, her arms folded protectively around a big black-and-white tuxedo cat, while our Hobo slept peacefully in his favorite corner of the couch.

Hobo would never know I'd hopped out of a hot bath

to save him from a trip to the pound. Our old fellow lived in his silent world a few more years, talking to us in his loud voice and enjoying the security of his home. The other tuxedo cat, too, lived out his life in the neighborhood. Because she hadn't met with success and had angered many neighbors, the Cat Police lady never again trapped cats. Her roses bloomed profusely, and I like to think the tuxedo cats had something to do with that.

Christian (Pat's nephew) and Hobo

Ziba's Tale

by
Susan Easterly

Ziba showed up on our doorstep on a wet, cold February evening. Returning from the grocery store, I pulled into the driveway as my four-year-old daughter burst out the front door with news: "We found a kitty!"

Even though I am a pet writer who loves cats, at that time in my life I did not have a cat—for a good reason. Our family had rescued Edo, an ex-racing Greyhound, who was extremely gentle. But he had been trained to chase small, furry objects. A Greyhound could catch a cat, and I didn't think anything good would come out of that combination.

We brought the young tortie-patterned kitten, roughly three months old and weighing a couple of pounds, out of the rain and into a spare bedroom. I explained to my two children that we couldn't keep her, and that we would try to find her owner. I knew she must have one, because she sported a flea color around her tiny neck.

The "lost cat" flyers went up the next morning, and

around the neighborhood we went, making inquiries along the way. Our friendly mailman said he thought he knew where she lived, just a few blocks away, and he would get back to us. Time went by and no one responded to our flyers, newspaper ad and shelter lost-and-found posting. When the mailman returned and stated the owner didn't want his wandering kitten back, I knew we had to take a different tack to find a good home for our houseguest.

In the meantime, keeping Edo from the kitten and the kitten from Edo proved challenging, especially with two young children around. I had to be careful, so very careful that my daily nightmare of "what if . . ." did not happen. I had to find a home for her quickly!

I asked friends to spread the word. Suddenly, the kitten began to display some unusual behavior. I thought, *Nah, she is too young. No way!*

Off to the veterinarian we went. "Yes, your cat is in heat. Yes, she is young but it happens," said the vet. An empty wallet and a day later, our newly spayed and vaccinated cat returned to our home.

A friend said she knew someone who wanted a cat. Soon after, our kitten was off to her new home with a single lady, who listened to our instructions and said she would take good care of her new charge. We were sorry to see the kitten go, but I knew a safe home would be better than our precarious one.

Case closed—or so I thought—when the doorbell rang two days later. I opened the door, and the kitten was thrust back into my arms. Her new owner ran back to her car, which had been left with its motor running, calling out, "My landlord won't let me keep a cat! Sorry!" The kitten, who appeared happy to be back, looked a bit smug.

What now? Feeling desperate and aware that the animal shelter already had too many cats that needed homes, I called our local pet supply store. I explained the situation and asked whether they might have space available to display an adoptable rescue kitty. The friendly voice on the phone said, "Sure, we do that. Bring her down." Putting the kitten in a cage for display was the last thing I wanted to do, but I truly felt it was for the best. Surely, someone would adopt our cute little cat. When I dropped off the kitten at the store, I assured her that everything would be fine, and then I left.

The next afternoon, I received a frantic phone call. "Please come and get your cat right away!" the now not-so-friendly voice said. "She hisses and threatens anyone who comes near her. She is ruining our store's reputation!"

"I'll be right there," I replied, grabbing my keys. Driving back to the pet supply store, I wondered if the sweet kitten I knew would now attack me, too. Was she so upset that she had been left there that she was lashing out at everyone?

At the store, I walked up to the cage, slowly opened the door and braced myself. The kitten jumped right into my arms and began purring. She looked at me with a this-has-been-fun-but-let's-go-home-now look.

The kitten and I returned home to cries of, "Can we keep her, Mom?! Can we?!" They had already thought of a name for her—"Ziba." I was warming to the idea of keeping her, but was still unsure of Edo's reaction to the newest family member.

It was time for the introduction. Though Ziba and Edo had been aware of each other for weeks, they had never met face to face. Holding the kitten, I also held my breath as the two sniffed each other, the pint-sized kitten and the 90-pound Greyhound whose nose seemed bigger than her head. When Edo got too close for

Ziba's comfort, a tiny paw swatted Edo's nose. He looked surprised and stepped away. It was a start, though I couldn't imagine ever leaving them alone together. *Would I always have to keep them separated?* I worried to myself.

In the end, Ziba solved my problem for me. One day, after returning home from running errands, I unlocked the door and saw that my worst nightmare had come true . . . or had it? There, on the carpet, lay Edo, calmly looking up at me. Between his paws snuggled tiny Ziba, sound asleep.

Ziba, who always knew where her forever home should be, lived with our family for more than 20 years. The cat we thought we could not keep remained best friends with Edo until the end of his life.

Ziba

Picture Perfect

by
Terri Elders

They rollicked into my heart right after we retired to the country: Groucho, Harpo and Chico, each silky, slinky feline sibling a tribute to its Marx Brothers namesake. But these mismatched triplets didn't earn any standing ovations . . . not from my husband, Ken.

When I worked in Washington D.C., I'd hurry home each evening, eager to leash up our purebred Akita, Tsunami, and scurry off to the dog park. Ken's dog by day, mine at night. But in our new home, those two became inseparable. They'd gaze at *Animal Planet* in the mornings, snooze through the afternoons and gambol around the lawn at twilight. Tsunami had become *man's* best friend. With no dog park to visit, I'd been excluded.

One day I spied a tub of kittens at a feed store, under a placard proclaiming, "Free Barn Cats . . . Guaranteed to Vanish Varmints." Our vacant stable had slots and stalls aplenty for a tabby to explore. And I'd certainly welcome a mouse-free house. I hurried home to tell Ken.

"No cat," he cautioned. "Tsunami will think it's prey. Or lunch."

"Come on. You've got your pet. I want a cat."

Ken shrugged as I headed back out the door. "OK, but don't expect me to pay it any attention."

I returned shortly, carrying a big cardboard box. The minute I walked into the house, Tsunami sprang up, pawing and snuffling. I rushed into the bathroom, dog at my heels. I slammed the door and opened the box. They meowed up at me, my three fetching fraternal triplets, two females and a male. I sat on the floor and snuggled them. They had such a clean scent, like line-dried linen.

Ken opened the door a cautious crack.

"Don't let Tsunami in," I warned.

"Three? Don't you think you overdid it?" Ken frowned, stepping inside. The trio sassed and spat, skittered off my lap and huddled behind the toilet.

"You know, Ernest Hemingway once said that one cat leads to another. So, I couldn't choose just one. They're triplets and absolutely irresistible. Don't you agree?"

Ken snorted. "I can resist them easily. Did you give them names?"

I pointed at the black and white one. "She's Groucho, tuxedo and all, like in *The Night at the Opera*, my favorite Marx Brothers movie."

I nodded at the fleeciest, the marmalade male. "This is Harpo. He's a tomcat. Remember those movies where Harpo Marx used to wear a red fright wig and chase the girls? This one loves to boss and wrestle with his sisters."

I picked up the remaining kitten, coal black except for glittering emerald eyes. "This is Chico, the tough one. The storekeeper said the people who brought them in told him she was a good mouser. In the movies, Chico always dealt with the neighborhood nuisances."

Ken shook his head, snickered and left, blocking Tsunami as she attempted to squeeze through the doorway.

That first week, the kittens remained sequestered in the bathroom with their food and water dishes, training themselves to their litter box. I still didn't trust Tsunami to recognize these were chums, not chow. She'd taken to camping in the hallway outside the bathroom, salivating whenever I opened the door.

"She needs her own pet," Ken finally said. He went to town and returned with Nat, a mixed-breed seven-week-old puppy. Tsunami, entranced, flopped down patiently so Nat could crawl on her back and gnaw on her legs.

The kittens grew quickly. With Tsunami preoccupied playing surrogate mom, they gained confidence and began to explore the house, sashaying from room to room. Tsunami occasionally lunged at them, but the kittens escaped by squishing out of reach under a sofa or table. Outdoors, if Nat gave chase, they'd scamper up a nearby tree. Ken continued to allude to all three as "he" or "him." They sensed his disdain and kept their distance.

As they morphed into full-sized cats, their personalities emerged. Groucho always craved center stage. Persistent and attention seeking, she'd wedge herself between me and the computer or me and my book. Harpo played pranks. He'd forage in the dogs' toy box, and later I'd discover a chew toy or ball in out-of-the-way crannies that the dogs themselves could not possibly reach. Chico, the hunter, perched atop the birdhouse or the basketball hoop, scanning the sky.

All three adored Nat, who allowed them to cavort around him and nuzzle his muzzle. Nat never turned down a pat or a rub from any creature. The cats still skirted around Tsunami, who'd snarl menacingly from time to time. Clearly, she, like Ken, regarded the triplets as nuisances to be tolerated, but never embraced.

Ken grumbled when they hopped onto the kitchen counter, growled when they knocked his glasses and pens from the game table to the floor, and grouched when they used the side of the carpeted staircase as a scratching post.

One evening, Ken took the dogs out for their customary evening stroll, Tsunami on her mandatory leash, Nat frisking along. He returned with a big grin. "Did you see the cats parading behind us, up and down the street?" He shook his head in amazement. Later, he announced that Chico, the reclusive cat, had sidled up to the side of his chair and had taken a test hop onto his left knee.

Another evening, I came home to find Ken napping in front of the blaring television, the dogs slumbering at his feet. Harpo dozed curled up in Ken's lap, while Chico and Groucho snoozed on either arm of his chair. I snatched my digital camera and captured the picture. Let sleeping dogs lie . . . and cats, too.

When Ken woke up, the cats had already departed.

"The cats took a nap with you," I said, "in your chair."

"No way!" he exclaimed. I produced the photo. Ken stared at it, and then chuckled with what seemed like a trace of affection.

Ken never warmed up to the cats completely. If he picked

up his reading glasses and they looked fogged, he'd claim the cats had sneaked onto the coffee table to lick them. The dogs, of course, never were blamed for anything. But, on frigid nights, my kind husband counted heads to make sure all animals—cats and dogs alike—were inside. Once, when I walked in from the kitchen, I glimpsed Ken patting Chico's head.

"She's such a good mouser," he said, looking embarrassed. I noted he'd said "she."

Evenings, the entire menagerie retired to our bedroom, dogs plopping down on both sides of the bed. On especially arctic nights, all three purring cats snuggled up to Nat. Tsunami, not surprisingly, avoided such group hugs. Sometimes the cats even nestled atop our quilt. If one occasionally dared to trample across my husband's chest, he'd reach out, snatch it up and deposit it onto the floor, never breaking the rhythm of his snores.

In my book, the cats deserved to take a bow. They were picture purr-fect, and I had that special photo to prove it. It's since disappeared. I think the jealous dogs ate it, but Ken would have claimed the cats did.

Harpo

Cat Mulan

by
Margie Yee Webb

What is that? I asked myself. I was looking out the living room window to the front deck. Standing on the deck was a creature I had never seen before.

Living in a house on hilly terrain surrounded by trees, grassy areas and other houses a short distance away, I have seen some wild animals around, mainly deer and turkeys. But this animal was different.

Is that a coyote? Or a fox?

After poking around the front part of the deck, the creature turned and raised its head in my direction. *Yes, a fox. It has to be a fox.*

Then I remembered that my cat—Mulan—was outside. I had let her out earlier that morning.

Where is she? Where's Mulan?

But the fox intrigued me more at that moment, so I grabbed my digital camera to snap a few shots of it. Knowing

Mulan, I wasn't too worried.

Mulan, a black tiger-striped tabby, was about six weeks old when she picked me—yes, picked me—when I was visiting the Front Street Animal Shelter in Sacramento. Not long after we arrived home, Mulan started exploring. She found the stairs and staked out a spot on one of the steps near the top. It was too cute and I had to snap a photo. Standing at the bottom of the stairs, I called to her and she posed perfectly for me. She loved the camera and the camera loved her.

That one moment launched my passion for taking photos of my cat. One of my favorite photos is one I took of her curled up in a ball of fur, head tilted to the side, showing off her big ears. I coined that photo her baby picture, naming it *Baby Love* after the song by The Supremes. Naturally, since Mulan was my first cat, I showed off that baby photo whenever I talked about her.

I took photos of Mulan when she was animated and playful, checking out a rolling toy and even a red onion. I captured her when she was meditative and thoughtful, sitting in a spot of sunlight or stretching out on the sofa. I caught her when she was enchanted and inquisitive, getting her first look at deer through a window. Mulan has personality!

Not long after, Mulan had her first of many adventures in the great outdoors. Although I was hesitant to let her outside, it was also a chance to take photographs of her in a different setting.

Mulan liked exploring her new surroundings. She checked out the front deck and must have studied it well, because one time, she made a mad dash across the deck, leaped off and landed on the roof of the garage, which was adjacent to the deck. She was like a cat on a hot tin roof.

Her first encounter with a deer was scary . . . at least for me. She got so close that she was practically dancing with the deer. The deer—a buck—took a stance, lowering his head with his big rack aiming down, and eyed Mulan. She, being the brave warrior, took her own stance, staring down the buck by staring up at him. The deer backed down. While this was happening, I managed to take some photos.

Another time, Mulan was literally talking to a buck and was so close to his ear, it looked like she was playing the deer whisperer. It was unbelievable—and I captured that moment on my camera. I wondered what she was saying, for the buck sure seemed like he was listening intently. Did Mulan give him food for thought?

It was a different story when it came to the turkeys. Most of the time, Mulan would stalk them from a distance. I heard that it could be dangerous if a bunch of turkeys were to surround a small animal, but that didn't ring true with Mulan. One time, I caught her playing hide and seek with a turkey. *Snap* . . . got that photo. My cat was both the crouching tiger and hidden dragon at the base of a tree as the turkey strutted by, seemingly oblivious that Mulan was in front of the tree. She sure surprised the turkey!

One bright sunny day, looking out my window, I could see a number of deer and turkey grazing on the hillside near the entryway of the home. Mulan was outside, but nowhere to be seen. Moments later, Mulan leaped off the entryway roof, landing in the middle of the deer and turkey, startling them all. While Mulan knows how to make friends, she also knows how to make mischief!

Having witnessed Mulan interacting with deer and turkey, I wondered how she would be with the fox, which was still on the deck. *Will she be fearless?*

I soon found out. The fox stepped off the deck and headed across the hillside by the entryway. Just as the fox strolled past a tree, Mulan emerged from behind the tree and pounced toward the fox. The fox was not fazed at all and it continued on its path.

I looked on in disbelief as Mulan followed. Worried, I opened the front door and stepped out onto the deck. Leaning over the railing, I saw the fox take a few more steps before stopping in its tracks to lie down in some weeds. Surprisingly, Mulan also stopped and did the same thing. There they were, both lying down, a short distance apart from one another.

Now what? I wasn't about to go up on the hillside to rescue Mulan—who knew what Mulan or the fox would do? Still armed with my camera, I did what I did best and snapped a few more photos before going back inside to stake out a different vantage point from the back of the house. When I got there, the two were still resting.

Suddenly, the fox got up, headed toward a wooden fence and climbed over it. Fortunately, Mulan didn't follow. Shortly, she got up and started toward the house. I met her part way, picked her up and brought her inside. I told her that was the last of her outdoor adventures, for then.

As you can well guess, I have captured many unique photos of Mulan. Her spirited, yet philosophical, nature inspired me to create a gift book of her photos, intertwined with words of wisdom and humor to complement the photos.

While working on the gift book, I decided that Mulan needed a stage name. Thus, she became "Cat Mulan." I wanted to be sure there was no confusion with the Disney film *Mulan*, which was based on a Chinese poem of a girl who disguised herself as a man to enlist in the army in place of her elderly father.

And it turns out that Cat Mulan is much like that woman warrior character. She is brave, fearless and oh-so adventurous, which will keep this kitty paparazzo forever on her toes!

Editor's note: Margie is the co-creator of *Not Your Mother's Book . . . On Cats*. To learn more about Margie, her gift book and Cat Mulan, please read her co-creator bio, found in the back of this book.

Cat Mulan being the "deer whisperer"

CHAPTER SIX

Pussies
Galore!

Just can't get enough . . .

The Transgendered Cat

by
John Reas

I always thought I had the coolest older sister around. Although seven years my senior, Mary was the kind of sister who was a natural leader and didn't seem to mind that a snotty-nosed first-grade kid like me would seem to materialize out of nowhere to pester her.

In short, Mary was the glue that held us together. She was the trailblazer and the spirited one in the family, and was never one to shy away from her responsibility that came with being the eldest. She was the one who could be counted on to organize snowball fights among us kids or to take us over to the neighborhood skating rink in the dead of winter. During the summer months, she was the one who Mom would rely on to round us up for supper or to arrange games of hide-and-seek at the park.

Mary was also the first among us to engage in what became the school rite of passage—the annual science fair. Her first project was to demonstrate the different parts of an animal's skeletal system, and for that, Dad managed to bring home a skeleton of a housecat from his research lab. Mary proudly took the skeleton to school and received a well-deserved "A" for her efforts. As a nod to Woody Allen's film debut, she even titled her project "What's New, Pussycat?" It was shortly after Mary's experience during the science fair that a real cat became a part of our lives.

Although dogs eventually became a major part of the home, our first family pet was feline. The year I was in first grade was the year that all five Reas kids happened to attend St. Mary's Parish School in Defiance, Ohio, at the same time. Mary, who was in eighth grade, was responsible for herding us the six blocks to school.

One afternoon, when we were coming home after school, Mary spotted an all-black stray that had scampered up to us. She reached down and scooped up the cat into her arms.

"Wow, Mary," said my sister Beth, "he seems to like you. I wonder who his owner is."

"He doesn't have a collar, and probably has no home," Mary replied. "Poor thing looks half-starved. Let's take him home. He needs some food."

As we trooped into the house, Mary proudly showed Mom what she had brought home.

"C'mon, Mom, you've always said that eventually we could have a pet," Mary said to Mom. "Look at this poor thing. He's the perfect addition to the family. Besides, I am an expert in cats now. I'll take great care of him. I promise." A trial lawyer couldn't have done a better job in making a case before a grand jury.

"All right, kids. We can keep the cat. But Mary, it's your

responsibility. Cleaning the litter box, feeding the cat, making sure it has water. Everything," stated Mom as she laid out the conditions for adopting the pet into our family. "However, we still need to post some signs in the neighborhood in case someone is looking for a lost cat."

When Dad arrived home, he was ambivalent about the pet, but also reiterated that we needed to post some signs around the area. A couple of us kids—under Mary's supervision—drew some "Cat Found" signs and taped them to light poles in the neighborhood. But after weeks with no response, we all reached the conclusion that the cat was meant to live with us.

Mary gladly took to her new duties as keeper of the cat. She made sure he was fed and watered and tended to the litter box, and, naturally, took the important step in naming him. Being raised in the 1960s, Mary was much more aware of the social turmoil that was going on around than her siblings were. She loved the music of The Beatles and Joan Baez, and some of her friends had older brothers who were fighting over in Vietnam. And even though he had already passed away and left his mark on history, Mary insisted on calling the cat "Malcolm" in honor of the late Malcolm X, who had already acquired legendary status by then.

Over the next several weeks, Mary and Malcolm became inseparable. He would jump into her arms and purr away to his heart's content whenever he heard her banging through the back door, with me and my older brother Bill and my sisters Cathy and Beth in tow.

Thanks to Mary's care, Malcolm started to build back his strength. I'm sure he was the predecessor to Morris—the famous finicky cat—as he had a preference for Friskies over any other brand Mary attempted to introduce into his diet. And the diet seemed to be working wonders, as Malcolm put on more and more weight.

That was, until that fateful Friday morning as we were getting ready for school. It was a sunny spring morning, and, as usual, there was the typical kitchen pandemonium as we began the day.

"Mom, I want to go over to Chris' house after school, OK?" asked Cathy.

Mom was about to respond when Bill said, "Oh yeah, Mom, I plan to go over to Charlie's this afternoon. Also, did you see my book report? Huh?"

Beth came into the kitchen and shouted, "Mom, I can't find my hairbrush! Have you seen it?!"

Not being able to get a word in edgewise, Mom quickly sounded off in her drill-sergeant voice. "No, no, no, and Beth, for the last time, no. You've got to keep up with your own stuff."

Then she addressed me. "John, put the Cap'n Crunch cereal away, because I'm making pancakes. Remember, kids, we're going over to Grandpa's for dinner this evening. So I want all of you back here right after school."

As the sound in the kitchen rose to a crescendo, Mary went to the utility room to check on Malcolm's food and water bowl.

"Mom, come quick! There's something wrong with Malcolm!" The panic in her voice was enough to send all of us running into the room to see what was going on.

There, on the floor next to the dryer, was a prone Malcolm, who was straining against something while mewing quietly.

Never at a loss for words, Bill shouted out, "What's that coming out of his butt?"

Cathy let out with a shriek, "Ewww, I think I'm going to be sick!"

Mom came in and with one look, grabbed Mary and said, "Quick, grab some blankets! Malcolm is about to have kittens."

Mary looked up. "Mom, that's impossible. Malcolm's a male!"

"Not anymore. He's a she!"

Mom took immediate command and shooed us all back into the kitchen, except for Mary.

"C'mon girl, you can do it," we could hear Mary as she quickly got her bearings in her newly found role as labor coach. "That's right. Good job, Malcolm. Atta boy. Sorry, I mean, atta girl."

For the next 20 minutes, we could hear her cheering Malcolm on while the cat let out an occasional screech. Finally, Mom called us back into the utility room. There, contentedly nursing away, were five kittens. Malcom licked each one clean.

"Wow, Mom, how did that happen?" I asked. "I didn't think boy cats could have babies."

Bill and Cathy immediately turned on me. "Malcolm was never a boy! Gee, don't you know anything?"

I was still confused. "What do you mean, he was never a boy? Of course he's a boy. Mom—Bill and Cathy are picking on me!"

Mom shushed us all. "Well, the joke's on all of us for not checking out that cat more closely! Just wait 'til Dad gets home!"

"But, we can keep them, right, Mom?" Beth asked. She

was looking forward to having a kitten of her own. "I mean, we will take good care of them. Look, it's perfect. There's one for each of us!"

"Like I said, kids, let's wait until your father gets home from work. Now, off to school, all of you, before you're late."

That day, we were the hot topic of the day at St. Mary's, as the story quickly spread about the miracle that occurred in the Reas household. Needless to say, Dad wasn't too pleased about the sex change that took place with Malcolm that morning, and over the weekend, he convinced his cousin—who owned a small dairy farm outside of town—to take Malcolm and her litter off our hands.

We were all crestfallen about Malcolm and the kittens' move until Dad came home the following week with a new German Shepherd. In the long run, the dog became a great family pet. And Dad also made absolutely sure that the dog wasn't anything but 100-percent pure male.

John and Mary

Stan and Ollie

by
Dianna Graveman

My two best friends and I, all young girls about 20 years old, had just moved out of our parents' homes. We were flushed with the heady excitement of being on our own and supporting ourselves. We all shared a quiet little home until one day, when Stan and Ollie moved into our lives.

We were never quite sure if "our two guys" were litter-mates or mere feline acquaintances. Like their comedian name-sakes—Laurel and Hardy—one was plump and colorful, the other long and pale.

Stan was a little short on cat brains and had a difficult time lapping water without snorting some up his nose, after which he would shake his head violently to clear his sinuses and whap his head on the wall. Fearing a kitty concussion, we placed his bowl in the center of the room.

Stan also had a hard time discerning between his litter box and our vinyl beanbag chair. We were forever cautioning houseguests to choose a "safer" seat. But Ollie found the situation amusing and often sat facing the beanbag chair with his tail swishing, waiting for some hapless victim to settle into the comfy seat following another of Stan's mistakes.

If Stan was the weak link, Ollie was the pick of the litter. He didn't get so round by meekly stepping back and claiming only his share. His appetite grew to epic proportions—and not just his appetite for food.

New to pet ownership, it hadn't occurred to my roommates and me that we ought to have Stan and Ollie neutered. It also hadn't occurred to us that since Ollie and Stan had simply wandered into our home one day, they might also simply wander out whenever they pleased.

One evening while we had guests, someone opened the door and in wandered Ollie, followed closely by Ollie Lite. The senior Ollie simply made himself at home with his little one as if he was sharing joint custody and it was his weekend with the kid. We made a vet appointment for the following week.

Life with our little cat-men was not easy. True to his weak-link status, Stan got sick often, and hefty vet bills were a monthly expense. The purchase of many great pairs of shoes was sacrificed for the good of one sickly cat. Each time, miraculously, we thought, Stan recovered to live another day and deposit his DNA in the beanbag chair once again.

All good things must come to an end, and so it was with Stan and Ollie. In spite of our efforts to curtail Ollie's social life until the date of his "procedure," he regularly continued to slip through our legs and out the door. Stan, a cautious homebody, usually stayed behind. Apparently, one day he wondered what he was missing and slipped out with his littermate. Ollie returned home that evening alone.

For a few days, Ollie wandered through the house, bereft and bewildered. He moved quietly from room to room, pausing each time he passed the beanbag chair for a brief memorial sniff.

Then he moved on—literally.

The last time I saw him, Ollie stopped moving long enough to shoot me a backward glance, daring me to deny him his freedom, before vanishing between two houses. Perhaps he had gotten wind of the upcoming vet appointment. I could almost hear the opening strains of Steppenwolf's *Born to be Wild* playing as the soundtrack.

Keep your motor runnin', Ollie.

A Great Idea

by
Ernie Witham

It all started when Bob—that's my cat—jumped up onto my computer keyboard and spelled out the word *jfassulfo-quonogen*. Oh sure, it doesn't look like much, but remember, he doesn't know the human alphabet. In cat language, that could mean, "Call me Ishmael."

Later that day, I saw the ad in *Parade* magazine: "CAT TV presents *Video for Cats*, guaranteed to stimulate the feline senses and help your cat live up to his full potential."

I began to think about *jfassulfoquonogen*. What if Bob was a wonder cat? An Einstein feline. What if Bob was—*gasp!*—Hollywood material?

I called the 800 number and they said it would be several days before I received *Video for Cats*, so I started rifling through my own videos, stumbling upon my collector's edition of *The Three Stooges Anthology*. I hesitated, and then a thought popped into my mind: *What about "The Three Cat*

Stooges?" Nah, animal slapstick was not in vogue. Besides, Bob didn't really get along all that well with other cats. His usual response was to chase them out of the yard then race around peeing on everything until he collapsed from dehydration.

I have it! A stunt cat. Sure. Hollywood must need stunt cats all the time!

I put Bob on the kitchen table. He leaped perfectly to the floor. I put a chair on the table. Another great leap. I got the ladder and dragged it out into the front yard, directly below the highest part of the roof. Bob was watching me from the kitchen window. In between licking his private parts and batting at a fly trapped between the window and the screen, he seemed genuinely interested in what I was doing.

Still something was missing. That's when I spotted the huge rubber band in the closet. A shiver of excitement raced up my spine. I opened the junk drawer in the kitchen and began a frantic search for the other piece I'd need. Finally, I found it.

"Look, Bob." I held up the little harness that had once been part of some kid's toy. Bob looked puzzled.

I smiled. "Or should I call you . . . 'Bungee Cat'?"

It was a perfect way to break into show business. We'd go to fairs, carnivals, local parks and even perform at cat shows.

I scooped Bob up into my arms and headed outside. I had already set up the video camera to record the event, so we quickly climbed the ladder to the roof. I could tell Bob was as excited as I was, because he began meowing the instant I put the harness onto his catnip mouse and tossed it over the edge of the roof for a test run. We watched as the mouse stopped 5 feet short of the ground and bounced up and down, up and down, up and down.

"See, Bob," I said. "Nothing to worry about."

I tied one end of the rubber band around the chimney and was just about to put the harness onto Bob when I heard a chirp.

Swallows. They must have nested under the eaves. Suddenly, there were dozens of them, darting about, trying to protect their young. I started swatting at them, but they just kept coming. Finally, when one of them almost hit me in the head, I took two steps back. Unfortunately, I was only one step away from the edge.

The rubber band actually stretched quite a ways before it broke, slowing my fall and giving me enough time to look down and see my wife's richly bloomed rose bush. I wondered briefly if I'd forever smell like an old lady at church. I laughed. Then the first of the thorns pierced my butt.

"Can I get you anything?" my wife asked, several days later. I was lying on the couch—on my stomach. She had actually been quite understanding about the rosebush. Of course, I had promised her a complete new rose garden when I pleadingly handed her a pair of thorn-removing needle nose pliers.

"No, I'm fine" I said. "But do we have to keep watching this tape? What about putting in *Video for Cats*?"

"Bob doesn't like that one," my wife said. "He only likes this one."

I watched the homemade video. And for the umpteenth

time, I saw myself falling, in slow motion, frantically grabbing for the pink rubber band. At the top of the screen, I could see Bob and half a dozen birds sitting on the edge of the roof watching my descent into the rosebush. The video stopped. Bob meowed at my wife, and she rewound it again.

"Oh, well," I said to my wife. "At least it stimulated his feline senses. Pass the icepack, will ya?"

Super Timmy

by
T'Mara Goodsell

The thing that surprised me the most about Timothy Kitty was the day he stalked a squirrel.

Our cats were used to squirrels. My sister and I began feeding Boo Boo, a friendly and hungry little red squirrel, by hand several years earlier. Boo Boo, it turned out, was a girl. So with a litter of mouths to feed, Boo Boo taught her babies to eat out of our hands, too.

Thus, the squirrels were our outside pets. Sometimes they would gambol up the side of the house and peer into the windows in search of their peanut distributors. One actually learned to knock on the door by jumping at the wrought iron scrollwork. Once, as I took in the sun, I felt a tail brush my leg and found two beady eyes pleading up at me from underneath the waffle design of my lawn chair.

And now, as I offered a salt-free peanut to a squirrel, I caught a peripheral glimpse of something in the shrubs—the cat. Timothy Kitty. His pre-pounce stance was unmistakable. Eyes saucer-round, his muscles tensed as he studied his field of attack.

I wasn't too concerned. Not only had Timothy's former owners had his claws removed, but I had seen him go after a squirrel once before. Just as he'd darted forward, the squirrel jerked up, as if attached to a string. But instead of running, she landed in a posture reminiscent of a sumo wrestler—and then held her ground.

As the cat neared, he apparently realized that the squirrel was only slightly smaller than he was. And if it wasn't running, didn't that mean that the little rodent possessed some hidden form of defense? Timothy then did a cartoon stop—the kind where he skidded then backpedaled in midair. At the end of the skid, he rebounded and rolled a bit, and then ungracefully landed not 2 feet from the squirrel, where he quickly propped himself upright and began to lick himself with an air of studied disinterest. Squirrel? What squirrel?

So I watched with mild amusement as little Timothy Kitty stalked his prey from under a shrub. He was playing tiger again, it was clear. Head down. Eyes focused. And then he shot out as if fired from a cannon.

But instead of stopping at the squirrel this time, he shot past. That was when I saw it. A dog had been stalking the squirrel, and Timothy was intercepting. He wasn't attacking the squirrel—he was saving it!

For one breath-stealing moment, I wasn't entirely sure what would happen. The dog was considerably bigger than Timothy, who put up a most heroic display of hissing and scratching with his clawless little feet. But surprise was in Timothy's favor, and this time, it was the dog's turn to back-pedal, cartoon-style, and run away.

The dynamics of the animal kingdom will forever amaze me. Timothy may not have been overly fond of the squirrels, but they were our squirrels, darn it, and nobody else was allowed to attack them. For one heroic moment, it was clear that Super Timmy protects his own.

Super Timmy

The Duck Channel

by
Risa Nye

When we were first married, my husband and I lived in a WWII-era fourplex on a busy corner in Albany, California—a small city next door to Berkeley. The bottom apartment on the left in the modest white clapboard house with green shutters was our home for four-and-a-half years. Although the place was tiny, we were comfortable there with just the two of us and our three indoor cats. We painted and decorated, kept its modest rooms neat most of the time, and enjoyed entertaining our friends and families.

We had a half-size apartment stove, which competed for space in the kitchen with the water heater, the refrigerator and place settings for the cats. In our dollhouse kitchen, all movements had to be carefully choreographed if we were to work together. We perfected the do-si-do maneuver necessary to pass from the corner sink to the stove as we chopped, washed or stirred. Storage space was at a premium—we sacrificed the cute drop-out-of-a-cupboard ironing board and turned its niche into a spice rack. The biggest and least practical horizontal surface was the deep triangular shelf that reached back from the tiled backsplash. A macramé plant holder, containing a spindly specimen reaching toward the only window, hung from a hook in the ceiling over the shelf.

The two of us began cooking together in high school and continued to feed our friends all the way through college and my husband's three years of law school. We'd make big pots of chili and pans of cornbread for our post-football-game parties, and actually used our crockpot—a standard issue wedding present in the 1970s. Another house specialty in those days was our famous spaghetti, always accompanied by crunchy garlic bread and lots of jug red.

Branching out a bit, we started experimenting with Chinese dishes, using a *Time Life* book (another wedding present). I made wonton soup from scratch, chopping by hand in those pre-food-processor days the pork, ginger and spinach for the filling, and then folding the wrappers, sealing them with moistened fingers and dropping them into homemade chicken broth. Our big wok, a wedding gift we had actually asked for, barely fit on the stovetop, but we used it often to stir-fry a variety of dishes.

Our menus grew in scope and level of difficulty, and we sought new challenges. Why not try Peking duck with Mandarin pancakes, scallion brushes and hoisin sauce—the whole deal? We purchased a fresh duck and then read step one of the recipe, which directed us to "loop a length of white cord under the wings," and then "suspend the bird from the string in a cool, airy place for three hours to dry the skin, or train a fan on it for two hours." Exploring our options for this part of the process, we took down the plant hanging over the shelf and hung up the duck.

We dragged out our electric rotisserie (a generous wedding present from a great aunt) and placed it on the shelf above the sink, directly underneath the dangling duck. This immediately blew a fuse, which meant we had to unplug whatever else was plugged in for the duration of the drying-out period. Plug in, blow fuse, repeat.

Meanwhile, juices from the duck hit the red-hot heating element below, producing a sizzling siren song for our cats. The three of them—Catrina, the calico with the crooked tail, Midnight, the skittish longhaired black cat, and sleek, gray Kinky Raoul—lined up and posed like ancient stone cats, their eyes glued upward to the flightless indoor bird. Six eyes narrowed to slits, an occasional ear twitched. If that duck had made a move, I am sure they would have jumped straight up in the air like cartoon cats. I don't know what was more amusing—the cats watching the duck or us watching the cats watching the duck.

After a couple of hours, the hapless duck was liberated from its noose and plunged into a boiling concoction of water, honey, ginger root and scallions. The cats used this reprieve to huddle together. I imagined them pooling their knowledge in order to calculate the precise amount of thrust and velocity required to leap up and take a whack at the duck, should such an opportunity present itself in the future.

Following its dip in the flavorful aromatic bath, the bird

was strung up again to twist slowly in the window for another couple of hours. Eventually, the cats sensed the futility of their duck watch. One by one, they crept off to find a square of sunlight somewhere, there to sleep and dream of indoor ducks, cooked and crispy, within their grasp.

Risa and Kinky Raoul

Talk to the Paw

by
Karin Frank

"Cats don't talk," my husband says.

I've given up trying to tell him that our cat, Nora, talks. The most expressive action he's ever seen her make is to stand in front of her half-empty food dish and look down into it.

I think she does this in an emphatic manner. I point this out to him.

"Emphatic," he repeats and chuckles indulgently. "You're stretchin' it."

I am sure that Nora has mastered at least a single word in English. That word is "noww."

"Noww." My husband laughs outright when I finally get up the nerve to tell him. "That's pretty close to a variation of meow, don't you think? You're stretchin' it again."

Nora only says "noww" when I don't move fast enough—to fill that half-empty bowl, to clean out her cat pan, to open a door for her. She ends the word "noww" with an upward inflection, giving it a subtle questioning effect. "See," that tone implies, "I am not seeking to command but to cajole." She accompanies this word with an impatient shaking of the right front paw and an upward tilt of her head.

This is different from the gesture that she makes with the left front paw that means, "Enough of this." That one looks like she has something stuck on the pad and is trying to shake it loose. The gesture is accompanied by a glance back directly over her left shoulder.

Nora can be quite diplomatic.

"Riiight," my husband says when I describe this to him, "Diplomatic."

"Riiight," is what he says after telling me that I'm "stretchin' it."

"Enough, enough," he complains when I praise Nora for having the gift of speech. And he makes a gesture as though something is stuck to the palm of his left hand.

"Well, maybe not," I say with a slight upward lilt to my tone at the end. I, too, can be diplomatic. "Maybe I'm only seeing and hearing what I want to see and hear."

Then one day, Millie came to visit. She is our neighbor's cat and she stays with us when the neighbor goes on a trip.

Millie makes a definite recognizable sound for spider— "ahh-ahh-ahh-ahh"—and shakes her paw. This means, "Get that thing out of here." Millie doesn't like spiders. She repeats this call, emphasized with her paw, until someone removes the offending arachnid. We have seen her do this many times, in our house and in our neighbor's.

Millie also says, "owwt," but she only says it while standing in front of the outside door. And as soon as it is opened, she exits.

Millie and Nora get along well. They stand by the door and say "noww" and "owwt" in chorus. I find this to be very effective. My husband ignores it.

The evening of one of Millie's visits, my husband and I sat down to dinner in the dining room. Millie, and then Nora, entered the kitchen and proceeded to eat from their respective bowls.

Apparently, a spider chose that moment to descend along his string toward the two cats. First Millie—and then again Nora, playing copycat—made the spider sound. I assume they shook their paws in our direction.

My husband rose from the table.

"Where are you going?" I asked.

"To get rid of that spider," he said.

"What spider?"

"The one bothering the cats."

I said nothing. I didn't bother to point out to him that he had responded exactly as he would have if the two cats had spoken.

"Riiight," he'd have said. "You're stretchin' it."

Millie

Freebie

by

JC Andrew

I should have known better. He was a cute kitten—gray-striped with white markings, small and thin and the last of his littermates. The pet store owner was very attentive when I hesitated in front of the almost-empty cage containing this scrawny leftover.

I was just moving away from the cage when he said, "We can't sell him because he's so small. He may need a little extra care. I'll give him to you if you would like to have him." That is when I should have turned and bolted for the door. I didn't, however, and thus Freebie came into our lives.

The kitten may have been free—the veterinarian care was not. Exams, shots, vitamins, tonics and a minor life-altering operation quickly ran up the size of my family's investment in this little "gift."

Because of all that care, Freebie did eventually thrive and grow into a strong-willed, independent cat that put our shepherd-mix dog in her place, especially at meal times. Freebie had enough wisdom to curl up with me when I sat to read or watch TV, ensuring he had the power elite on his side. If our dog also wanted some human attention, she could have just a little, but only if deference were shown to the alpha male, who was one-third her size.

Freebie was allowed to wander outside, bedecked with a bell on his collar to give birds and other little animals a warning of his approach. One day he must have thought a meal of squirrel was within reach. We found Freebie 30 feet up a tree in our front yard. Applauding his climbing ability, we called him to come home. It was then we found that what goes up does not necessarily come down.

All day we kept calling to Freebie, and that evening, we put his dinner under the tree. We could see he was tempted to come down, but he chose to stay where he was. At dark, with the hope that a night in the open would make Freebie reconsider his position, we reluctantly went inside.

The next morning, nothing had changed. The water, food and cat were still frozen in time. Using our most inviting voices, we again entreated Freebie to come down. He would have none of it, although he did have a few comments to make about the discomforts of his location. The situation had all of us worried.

The third day, we were desperate. We couldn't leave Freebie in the tree until he dropped out of it from hunger. It was at this time I learned that all those sweet, grade-school stories are a lie—the fire department *does not* rescue cats from trees! We eventually called a tree service. They would be very happy to help—at our sizable expense. By late afternoon, a man arrived, put on his tree-climbing equipment, wrapped a rope around the tree and ascended.

Was Freebie grateful? Of course not! He simply clawed his way higher into the branches. Fortunately, his rescuer was a better climber. A few scratches to the rescuer and a generous check from us later, Freebie was back on ground-level and safe in our house.

Freebie's roaming time thereafter became shorter, better supervised and mostly on the ground. He must have heard my husband's promise that he would, "have a new home if his *up* was ever again not matched with a *down*."

About this time, I became aware that my pet-store bargain had given me a special gift. My eyes often itched, and my face was puffy. I had developed an allergy . . . to cats.

In spite of having to wash my hands every time I petted him, life with Freebie was uneventful until the afternoon he disappeared into the woods behind our house. We hunted and called for him, but were having no luck until we heard a frustrated *meow*.

As one, we looked up. High in the branches crouched Freebie, no doubt wondering why it was taking us so long to call the nice man to get him out of this mess.

That did it! My husband marched to the house, returning with the garden hose, complete with nozzle. Aiming the water high into the tree above the stranded climber, he presented Freebie with a choice . . . come down or get very wet. Freebie had met his match. After several moments of damp consideration, he decided that he could, indeed—

with sufficient encouragement—descend unaided from his lofty perch.

I wish I could say we all lived happily ever after. I suppose, in a way, we did. Our family never had to worry about the cat again because my husband offered him—once again, as a freebie—to a secretary who was delighted to get such a bargain. Best of all, he stayed out of trouble—because there were no trees in his new person's yard.

Jinxed

by
Lisa Tognola

He passed the interview with flying colors.

"Why do you want to live with us? What challenges are you looking for? Where do you see yourself in five years?" We asked some tough questions and he had all the right answers, responding to each question with a confident *meow*.

He was deliciously cute and wonderfully fluffy. When he arched his little back, pounced on five-year-old Elizabeth's shoes and untied her laces, we decided this playful kitten was perfect for our family. We also decided to start double knotting our shoelaces.

"We'll take him," I told the animal shelter worker.

The gray tiger-striped kitten that we named "Jynx" was affectionate and curious and explored every nook and cranny of our house. My kids played with him, cared for him and loved him. Jynx returned their love by guarding oldest daughter Heather's room at night, providing a wake-up pounce upon Henry in his bed each morning and continuing to untie Elizabeth's shoelaces whenever possible.

But despite the unconditional love he received, Jynx became restless as an indoor cat. Not satisfied with the confines of our home, he constantly scratched at the door, yearning for a taste of the great outdoors. Beckoned by the call of the wild, Jynx longed to enter our yard where he could be free to scamper after squirrels, frolic near the creek and attend school.

Yes, attend school. From the moment we allowed him access to the outdoors, Jynx accompanied my son to grammar school. Like a four-armed bodyguard, he would amble alongside Henry until they reached the school grounds. Jynx would paw at the big red school door, hoping to gain entrance, until the principal would point to the "No Pets on School Grounds" sign and send him on his way. At three o'clock in the afternoon, Jynx would return to school to escort Henry home.

We worried about Jynx, knowing that by spending time outdoors, he was more vulnerable to dangers such as vicious dogs, threatening raccoons, street traffic, the harsh elements of winter and even school bullies. But we remembered the adage, "If you love something, set it free," and prayed for his safety. We worried most when Jynx was gone for days on end, especially since he tended to be naively trustworthy and often sat in the middle of the street, not understanding that he was a dark cat camouflaged against black asphalt.

One Saturday morning, a neighbor called to tell us Jynx was down on Weston Avenue. "He'll find his way home. He always does," I said to her. An hour later, I drove down Weston and spied a striped gray cat lying in the middle of the road. "Jynx!" I laid on the brakes. I ran to him but it was too late. I knew my children would be devastated to learn their young cat had been killed by a hit-and-run driver.

Picking him up carefully, I took him home and broke the news. Later that day, I returned to look for Jynx' identification collar, which had undoubtedly flung off upon impact. I found nothing. Back home, we placed Jynx in a cardboard box and buried him in the backyard in a hole that was 3-feet deep.

We had just begun the memorial service when Henry interrupted. "Just a minute," he said and disappeared into the house. Thinking he needed time to compose himself, we were surprised when he quickly returned and tossed something into the shallow grave. We heard a small *thud*.

"There's Elizabeth's sneaker, I know it was your favorite," he said earnestly to Jynx, gazing down at the box. Elizabeth started to open her mouth in protest, but changed her mind. Leaning on our shovels, we rested a moment, each of us reflecting on our short time with Jynx.

"I loved how he took walks with us like a dog," said Heather.

"I loved him even though he drank out of the toilet," Henry declared.

"I loved those shoes," said Elizabeth.

After the service, we went back inside and lit a memorial candle on the mantelpiece.

Later that afternoon, our neighbor popped over and, unaware of our loss, casually mentioned, "Jynx is on my back deck."

"What?!" we replied in unison. Our eyes immediately traveled to the gravesite, searching for any sign of disturbance, but we saw none. We peered toward our neighbor's house and observed Jynx trotting over to us. We went wild, hugging and kissing him. He took it all in stride, oblivious to the fact that until that moment, we had been convinced that he had lost one of his nine lives.

"But if this is Jynx, who's in the . . . ?" Heather inquired, pointing to the grave.

We shrugged and looked at each other in bewilderment.

To this day, we don't know whose cat lies in our backyard, only that we gave it a proper burial. We memorialized the grave as the "The Tomb of the Unknown Cat."

We confined Jynx to the house after the "incident." After all, this time we had been witness to one of the fateful dangers of outdoor cat life—cat versus car. But listening to Jynx' familiar scratching at the door day after day made it clear to us that it wasn't enough to offer him freedom from life in an animal shelter. We needed to allow him the freedom to explore life.

So we let him outside again. And although we constantly worry about Jynx and receive phone calls regularly from concerned neighbors, we have the satisfaction of knowing that our cat is contentedly enjoying the best of both worlds. One shoelace at a time.

Jynx

Cat-astrophe!

Mishaps, surprises and mayhem—oh, my!

The Secret Lives of House Cats

by
Roselie Thoman

I once thought that if my fluffy, white kitty had to hunt for his meals, he would surely starve. His days consisted of lazing in the sunshine and he filled his evenings with restful napping to make up for all the lazing he'd done earlier. Yes, there was some eating and chasing and pouncing, but a hunter he was not.

One evening, my husband, Matt, described a show he'd seen on TV.

"Hey, you know what? They did this experiment where they put little cameras on top of cats' heads to see what they do during the day."

"Oh yeah? See a lot of sleeping?"

"No! They got all this footage of house cats that are all lazy when they're inside, but then they go outside and turn into extreme, vicious hunters."

"Oh, come on," I'd said, looking over at Toshi lounging on

the couch and grooming his long, white fur. Sure, once spring arrived he plumped up a bit, but we figured the neighbors were being generous.

"Yup. Turns out all these little house cats are just as good of hunters as their cousins."

Toshi squinted up at me, stretched luxuriously and continued grooming.

"Yeah, well, Toshi wouldn't want to mess up his fur," I'd replied.

Toshi is adorable. After several months of marriage, I was able to talk Matt into bringing him home from the pound. My persuasive argument was that since Matt was going to be gone at police training for 10 weeks, I obviously needed some company. Over the years, Toshi has survived the addition of a hyperactive yellow Lab and two new humans. Toshi didn't seem to mind our dog too much, but when we brought our daughter home from the hospital, he was dismayed over the new lap arrangements. He would pretend she wasn't there and attempt to sit on her while she nursed.

It was always fun watching Toshi outdoors, trying to catch birds and squirrels. He would chase a squirrel up a branch and stalk around the tree's base. The squirrel would chatter at him while treed, but we were more concerned that the squirrel might realize he could take Toshi than we were of having to see the squirrel turned into lunch.

Toshi didn't have much better luck going after birds. He'd wait and watch a group of birds pecking at the ground for seeds or worms. He'd wiggle his rump and pounce, only to have them fly away with plenty of time to spare. As far as we could tell, his hunting skills were lacking.

One day, that all changed.

My children, Cali and Sawyer, were both napping. Matt was working nights and slept all day. I was enjoying the rare quiet of a successful triple nap and, to celebrate, I opened the sliding glass door to the deck and cleaned up the house. There had been a screen door as well, but our dog had run through it the previous week and Matt hadn't put it back up yet. I was OK with the risk of letting in a couple of flies in exchange for the fresh, summer air.

If those were the only critters entering, it would have been fine.

I was in the middle of picking up stuffed animals, wondering how they multiply so fast (What do they DO at night?), when I saw Toshi out of the corner of my eye. The last time I saw him, he'd been stretched out on a lounge chair in a pool of sunshine. He stepped over the threshold and into the dining room.

In his mouth, dangling from both sides like some grotesque mustache, was a giant, black snake.

"AHHHHHHHHH!" I screamed. I figured Matt, being a highly trained police officer, would be at my side within moments.

Toshi looked up at me with his bright blue eyes. Maybe he was proud. Maybe he was showing off his catch. All I could see was the wiggling body of the snake. Wasn't this Toshi, the cat who couldn't catch a five-legged spider if he tried?

No sounds from the back of the house. I was happy I

hadn't woken the children, but where was Matt? Clearly, snake eradication was within the husband's jurisdiction. I'm all for equal rights and whatever, but there are some things I am completely fine with, like a man kicking a live snake out of my home.

I couldn't take it anymore. Every second that passed was an opportunity for Toshi to get further inside and for the snake to wriggle free. I crept toward Toshi, careful not to startle him and cause him to drop his prize. I shooed him out, only coming as close as necessary as the snake was still trapped in his jaws. After that, I slammed the door shut and sat on the couch.

Soon, Cali and Sawyer were crying and ready for me to get them out of bed. Once up, I read books to them, but my skin was crawling and I was still a little disturbed that my scream did nothing to rouse Matt. While reading *The Belly Button Book* for the third time in a row, I wondered what would have happened if I hadn't been right there when Toshi came inside. I pictured Toshi dropping his catch and it slithering freely throughout the house. Would it have escaped, only to be found in the middle of the night, creeping up my pillow?

Later that day, I told Matt that maybe there was something about that video camera thing.

"Oh, yeah. Why?" he asked, still waking up.

"Because Toshi brought a snake into the house. That's why I was yelling this afternoon."

"You were yelling? Toshi brought a *what* into the house?" I told him the story of the day's events.

I wouldn't have believed it if I hadn't seen it for myself. Perhaps our furry little feline friends are more formidable opponents than originally thought. Plus, sleeping cops aren't much of a defense.

Toshi

Caught in the Sack

by
Roger Riley

The snap of the magazine into the chamber of the handgun echoed in the bedroom. I don't know which was louder, the thud of my rapid heartbeat or that loud snap.

As I cautiously looked around the room, I had one of those quick flashbacks they say you have when you are about to die. Only this time, it wasn't my past life that flashed before my eyes. Instead, in an instant, I reviewed the previous few hours that had brought me to this moment in time.

Cali, our beautiful, pudgy, longhaired calico and Maine Coon mix and Scruffy, our medium-haired, svelte black-and-white tiger, were our alarm clocks. Each morning at the break of daylight, "our girls" crawled all over my wife and me until we grudgingly got out of bed. Our morning routine was pretty much set from that point on, with my wife eventually leaving for work and me heading out to the coffee shop to catch up with the guys.

This particular morning, when I returned to the house after my absence of about three hours with my friends, I went upstairs to check my email messages. That's when I noticed Cali cautiously following me into the office with her plump body close to the ground. She slowly crept closer to my desk chair as I acknowledged her presence.

We call Cali our hippy cat because she is always so mellow. I found myself looking at ears, which were laid back, and her tail, twitching in every direction. Her worried eyes darted left then right. I could see the fur on her back ripple as tremors coursed through her body. That caused me to pause in reflection and concern.

As I pondered Cali's unusual behavior, we both heard a movement to our left. Cali immediately stopped still and went on point. I looked down to see Scruffy wedged under my printer table, which only has a 3-inch ground clearance, anxiously peering out. She was never mellow. In fact, as a seven-week-old kitten adopted at the same time as Cali, Scruffy was so frightened by her first reflection of herself in our full-length mirror that she hunched up on the balls of her feet, her hairs stood on end and her green eyes grew round as saucers as she hissed loud and long while dancing sideways away from the "intruder." She never quite got over that. To this day, Scruffy always has a look of impending attack on her face and every unexpected noise means there is something in the house that is going to get her.

At that moment, I multiplied the terrified look on Scruffy's face by 10 and I didn't like the answer I got. Our girls always slink around and hide when strangers come to visit. With both of them acting so weird, I realized that there had to be an intruder in the house!

I quietly eased back out of my chair and went to our bedroom where I kept our handgun. Cali was right on my heels, still moving in her low-slung, 'possum-looking crawl. I quietly removed the gun from my nightstand drawer. That's when I loaded the magazine into the gun.

Now, at the end of my flashback, I had to make a decision as to where to start looking for the intruder or to dial 911. I was just about to look under the bed when Cali and I both had the daylights scared out of us. Scruffy hurtled into the bedroom at breakneck speed, slid across the hardwood floor when she tried to slow down and slammed into the wall.

At the speed she was traveling, all I saw was a streak of black and white. Except I saw more white than black. Scruffy was accompanied by a noise that sounded like the loud, continuous, crackling rustle of a pile of dead leaves.

Upon hitting the wall, Scruffy immediately jumped up and turned to make another terrified beeline back out the bedroom door. At that exact moment, I made a grab for her and managed to snag a handful of plastic grocery sack! Cali—who must have been just as startled as I was—had long-since disappeared into another room. With a sigh of relief, I removed the magazine from my gun and replaced it in the nightstand.

As kittens, our girls had started a habit of tipping over small trashcans around the house. We always kept extra plastic grocery sacks under the used sacks in the cans so that when we would empty them, we could pull out the old one and shake in the new one. Somehow, when Scruffy turned over a trashcan to play with the contents, the handles of the grocery sack got tangled around her hind legs. She must have been running all over the house trying to dislodge the sack that wouldn't let go of her, for who knows how long. Additionally, Cali, having no idea what in the world was happening, probably ran all over the house with Scruffy, trying to fix the situation or get away from it, as was her habit whenever Scruffy was in distress.

When my wife came home a few hours later, I told her the story of my morning. After we both laughed until tears rolled down our faces, she asked where our girls were. I wasn't sure, as I had seen neither hide nor hair of the two since grabbing the sack off Scruffy. That day, we were due to leave on a weekend trip. I was told, in no uncertain terms, that we would not leave until we knew how the girls were doing.

We began looking for them in all their hiding places, with no luck. Finally, we found our pudgy Cali under the clothes dryer, wedged into a 4-inch-deep french drain. I had to tilt the machine forward in the cramped space of the laundry room so my wife could reach behind it to grab a part of Cali to get her out.

As I tilted the dryer forward more, Cali moved under it further, making it almost impossible for my wife to reach her. And I couldn't put the dryer down or it would squash the cat. With one final heroic tilt, my wife was able to snag Cali and scooped her into her arms. Our mellow, hippy cat was so frightened by the whole ordeal that my wife could feel violent tremors rippling through Cali's body in continuous waves.

Scruffy was a little easier to find—she was in her favorite hideout under my recliner. I reached in and pulled her out. But when I tried to set her down, she fought tooth and nail to stay right where she was, secure in my arms. Needless to say, we didn't get away for our trip on time, as we spent a while consoling our scaredy cats.

It's been over a year since the grocery sack fiasco with the girls. For the longest time, whenever we would handle a plastic grocery sack or shake open a garbage bag, the sound would make our girls run for cover. It's only been in the past two months that one or both of the cats have been tilting trashcans again. I never thought it could happen twice, but it did. This time the grocery sack caught Cali and the race was on!

Roger and the cats

One Honey of a Cat

by
Susan Guerrero

Honey Cat came into our lives after two years of heavy lobbying on the part of our 14-year-old daughter. We lived in Arizona then. My husband and I didn't want a pet cat and she did.

As a matter of fact, she wanted one deeply and passionately. She begged, pleaded and stated her case in writing, telling us all the ways a cat would enhance our family.

The more I decried how expensive animals could be, the more she dug in her heels. Finally, when friends of our children announced that their cat had kittens, the lobbying for a cat became intense and relentless. At long last, my husband and I gave in.

Into our lives came a tiny, squirming ball of fur that fit snugly in the palms of our hands. Her soft fur was the color of honey and she was appropriately named.

The little kitten charmed everyone in our family and we all fell madly in love with her, frisky antics and all. She loved climbing up our Christmas tree, after we festooned it with lights and breakable balls. When one of them smashed into smithereens on the floor, Honey Cat would look down at the shards, stick her head up in the air and calmly walk away.

The years flew by and Honey Cat became quite the huntress of the desert. She proudly brought all of her booty home to our backyard. Bunnies, mice, prairie dogs and all kinds of wildlife were fair game.

One fine afternoon, I left our patio door open. Honey Cat decided to get a bit more brazen and bring the day's catch into the living room.

As long as I live, I'll never forget what happened next. I was in the living room and looked over at Honey Cat. Her jaws firmly grasped an iguana lizard. It was longer than the entire length of Honey Cat's body.

Out of my mouth came a blood-curdling scream that scared even me. It emanated from deep inside of me. Honey Cat's ears flew back at the sound and she opened her mouth, depositing the lizard onto the living room floor. The desert creature was still very much alive and meandered underneath our couch.

My daughter came in to see what all the commotion was about. Her by-then-hysterical mother just pointed to the bottom of the couch.

"Oh, my goodness!" yelled my daughter when she spotted the lizard. "That's huge!" Being a quick thinker, she ran out of the room and came back in, carrying the broom and a large cardboard box.

Meanwhile, I was standing on top of the cushions of a

nearby loveseat. No way were my feet going to hit the floor with the lizard so close by.

My daughter stuck the broom handle underneath the couch, coaxing the lizard out. When he finally started crawling over the living room floor—*wham!*—she plopped the cardboard box over him.

Somehow, she got the box-covered lizard over to the patio door, lifted up the box and the lizard quickly crossed the patio, darting into the side yard.

Honey Cat, by the way, was totally oblivious to the disruption she caused in our household. She was making it known very loudly that she was ready to eat her tuna fish. Guess all the excitement made her a bit hungry.

Another time Honey Cat scared the wits out of us—and there were many such times—was when we feared for her very life.

She loved to go outside, even though we lived in a desert climate. There were many things in the wild that could hurt her, but Honey Cat thrived on adventure.

One afternoon, my daughter came running into the house. She was gasping.

"Mom! Mom! Something's wrong with Honey Cat!"

I ran out to the patio with her and saw Honey Cat. She was making a horrendous noise, a long, drawn-out, high-pitched moan.

"Go get the cat carrier," I said. "We've got to take her to the vet's."

Somehow, we got the wailing creature into the carrier, placed it on the back seat and drove quickly to the vet's office, which, luckily, was nearby.

We remained in the waiting room while the doctor looked over Honey Cat. When he came out to talk to us, the expression on his face was very serious.

"Honey Cat has been bitten by a snake," he said. The problem was, no one knew if it had been a rattlesnake or not. If it was, the bite could be deadly. Anti-venom treatment for such a bite would start at about $800, an amount we would not be able to afford.

The doctor saw the woeful looks on our faces and said he could start Honey Cat on an antibiotic regime, but she would have to stay at the veterinary hospital. He cautioned us, however, that if the snake had been a rattler, our beloved pet would probably not make it.

The next few days were touch and go. Honey Cat survived, however, and that's all we cared about.

We finally got the phone call to come pick her up. Honey Cat, though shaved where the snake piercings were, looked as frisky as ever. She was tearing her way out of the cat carrier on the way home in the car, so it was going to be hard to keep her in the house for the next week or so.

We suspect she was bitten by a snake underneath a shed that was attached to our house. Honey Cat loved to crawl under that shed. She never was bitten again by a snake, much to our relief.

We moved cross-country from Arizona to Massachusetts and Honey Cat, of course, came with us. She went from the heat of the desert to the "Arctic Tundra" of New England winters. She's adjusted amazingly well. Must be part of her 999 lives!

These days, Honey Cat is a very old cat. Has she settled

down to live a peaceful life? No way. Just recently, I heard the screaming sound of cats fighting.

"Thank heavens Honey Cat is upstairs," I said aloud. Looking through the glass top of our kitchen door, I peered into the backyard. I saw the two cats going at it and one was Honey Cat. She wasn't upstairs after all.

Her attacker was much bigger. He was probably the neighborhood bully. I flew out onto the porch, picked up an empty brass planter and hurled it at the fence near the two sparring cats.

That gave Honey Cat the opportunity to fly like a bullet across the backyard, up the back steps, through the open door and into the kitchen.

Little did I know, but that the bully cat had clawed Honey Cat good. When she stopped eating for four entire days, I called our veterinarian and expressed my extreme worry. She said to bring Honey Cat in.

The vet said Honey Cat had a fever and a huge abscess on her lower back that had to be drained. It was not a pretty sight, even though the doctor gave her lots of medication.

Honey Cat showed that—grandmother-age or not—she was still quite a fighter. The doctor called in an assistant to help hold her down. She ended up clipping Honey Cat's nails, too, because the assistant was running the risk of being shredded.

After antibiotics, an IV, a renewed rabies shot, tranquilizers to calm her down and paying a hefty veterinary bill, we finally took Honey Cat home.

I was so happy she was alive that I couldn't help crying. Tears ran down my cheeks as I nestled Honey Cat in my arms.

Within a few days, she was eating ravenously again, drinking and crying at the door to go outside. Before I let her out nowadays, it's imperative to scan the backyard for the big brawny bully cat. So far, so good—he has not been around.

Last time I looked, Honey Cat was snugly sleeping on the back porch, soaking the sun into her honey-colored fur.

She's the cat who has 999 lives. This lizard-toting feline survived a snakebite, a cross-country airplane ride and a major fight with the neighborhood bully cat.

Long live our beloved Honey Cat.

Honey Cat

Unwanted Surprises

by
Janice Singer

When it comes to surprises, most of them in our house are from a 13-pound crazy feline whom we lovingly refer to as "Georgie." Being a cat, Georgie dearly adored bringing lizards and buzzing insects into our home, and those presents I can deal with just fine, thank you. However, the new unwanted surprises he brought to me started about four summers ago.

One sunny humid Florida afternoon, I was in my office working at the computer when I heard that guttural Siamese cry-like-a-baby meow from inside the middle of the house. Suspecting something was amiss, I rose from my chair, gingerly rounded the corner into the dining room and hesitantly scanned the upcoming scene as I approached the living room. Everything seemed OK until . . .

"Oh, my God!" I said. Right in the middle of our living room was a black snake, all coiled up, with Georgie standing proudly to the side. I screamed as I ran for the nearest phone to call my husband, Jeff.

Upon hearing Georgie's newest catch he had drug through his cat door, Jeff said, "Just get the broom and dustpan, sweep it into the pan and take it out into the backyard."

"Are you kidding me?! You think I'm going to get my hand that close to the snake by holding onto an itty-bitty dustpan?"

"You're going to have to get it out somehow, and I can't come home from work."

"I'm not gonna touch that snake! You know snakes terrify me. And what if he moves? What if he goes under the couch?!" I can't be entirely positive, but I'm pretty sure that I heard muted chuckling on the other end of the phone.

"OK, I'll call Mom and Drew to see if they're home. But I guarantee Drew will not touch it. He *hates* snakes," Jeff said. "Mom won't mind doing it. Just throw a sheet over it for now. The snake will stay under there. It's probably more scared of you than you are of it."

"Not hardly," I retorted.

Having the assurance that my in-laws were on their way, I mustered up an extreme amount of courage to climb over the couch to get around the snake and to the linen closet. I grabbed a sheet, threw it over the snake and stood guard to make sure it didn't slither out.

Once my in-laws arrived, Drew confirmed he wasn't going to touch the snake, either. However, Jackie—Jeff's mom—had no problem scooting that snake into a dustpan and out the door, depositing him in our backyard.

With the snake out of the house, I could finally breathe.

But unless it slithered a mile away, it was still too close for my comfort. What was even worse was that I would never live down the fact I made my 72-year-old mother-in-law come get the unwanted visitor out of the house.

Sadly, this is not the end of the story. Apparently, Georgie had become the snake wrangler of our street. I've lost count of how many snakes he has brought into our humble abode. That summer, I was forced to quickly devise a list of friends and family to help with snake removal. Unfortunately, it was a short list.

There was the time Georgie dropped a snake at my feet at the bathroom door—I called my husband's friend after jumping over the snake, sweeping him into the bathroom with the broom and then shutting the door.

With the next snake, I asked the neighbor boy Nathan for help, much to his chagrin, as he was another snake hater. But, nonetheless, he was my gallant knight in shining armor and got the snake out. For the next snake, Nathan was again unlucky to be home, so he was quickly recruited and did the job.

By Snake #5, I was beginning to feel guilty about asking Nathan to help. Since it appeared that snake hunting was going to become Georgie's full-time job, I knew I would have to start learning to deal with the slithering menaces by myself.

But what about Jeff? Was he ever home during the snake invasions? That would be no, never, not at all, not even once. Thus, it became my problem to solve.

And I was proud of myself. I had gotten to the point where I could grab the broom—not the dustpan—and literally sweep the snake out the door into our carport. I didn't stop there either, sweeping the snakes almost all the way out into the street.

The first time I accomplished this mission by myself, I called Jeff and his reply was, "You didn't hurt the snake, did you?"

"If I'm lucky, I did."

"Honey, you can't kill snakes. They're harmless. And they eat rodents."

"Still don't care. Hopefully, I stunned it," I answered.

Georgie, blessedly for me, took a two-year hiatus from his snake-wrangling job. Or maybe all the snakes heard the warning from their snake cousins not to go near our yard. But last summer, it started again. The only saving grace I have is that Georgie still gives me that Siamese cry to let me know he's brought me a present.

I can hardly wait for this summer.

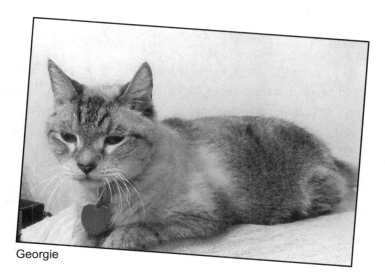

Georgie

Love Conquers Wall

by
Rieva Lester

At 17.6 pounds, my Gizmo is not going to win any games of hide-and-seek. Not that he'd want to anyway.

With the personality of a people-pleasing lap dog, Gizzers is the most sociable kitty I've ever met. When we have visitors, he becomes a Walmart greeter. And when my daughter and I come home, he races out to tell us how much he has missed us. But that spring night, he was nowhere to be seen.

We'd had construction crews in and out of our house for days, replacing our faulty pipe work. Gizmo already had given them the slip once—and he returned a walking mud bog, his once-silky coat replaced by a matted marsh.

I feared he'd gotten out again.

But then I heard it. The unmistakable muffled meow of my fluffy Giz. *Mrrrrrfff-eeeeooow.*

"Gizzers, where are you?" I called.

Mrrrrrfff-eeeeooow.

I checked the bedrooms, the bathrooms, the utility room, the garage.

Mrrrrrfff-eeeeooow.

I checked the crawl space, the front door and the sliding glass doors. Our two dogs scratched and whined from outside, pleading for me to let them in. "We'll help, Mom," they seemed to say.

Mildly interested, Gizmo's two feline brothers joined my Great Gizmo Hunt. They didn't have much to say. But Giz did.

Mrrrrrfff-eeeeooow.

Deep down, I already knew where Gizzers was. *Couldn't be,* I thought to myself. *That doesn't happen in real life, only in cartoons and comic strips.*

I hurried back into the main bathroom. "Gizzers?! Where ARE you?!" His cry wasn't quite as muffled this time.

MMMMEEEEOOOOWWW! he wailed.

I raced to call my dad, because that's what you do in an emergency. "Dad?! Would you please come up? I need you to cut my cat out of my wall!"

Stunned silence. "You're kidding," he said.

I wasn't.

The construction crews had Sheetrocked my very large Gizmo inside the very still-drying wall behind our shower.

My eight-year-old daughter Raegan fought back tears as we waited for her papa to show up. I fought back laughter. Or anger. Or both.

My dad and brother showed up within minutes. They cut a large escape hole for my Giz, but a wall stud blocked the exit. They cut a smaller hole on the other side.

I coaxed my big boy to the hole in the wall. In a move that defied his nine years and 17-plus pounds, Gizzers scrambled out the smallish rectangular opening. FREEDOM! But he wasn't in the mood to celebrate just yet. He needed to go potty—NOW! He did his business before returning to give me a hefty dose of thank-you nuzzles. Then he headed straight to his food dish.

I'm still not sure how my long-haired orca snuck past the workers. *How did they not see him? Not hear him?* I may never know.

The construction crews returned a few days later to patch up the holes from the Great Gizmo Rescue—at no charge, of course. After they packed up and left, I was relieved to find my Giz wandering in the hall instead of a wall.

Gizmo seems to have recovered nicely. And I haven't seen any evidence of PTSD—post-traumatic Sheetrock disorder.

Gizmo and Rieva's daughter Raegan

Mischief's Bath

by
Mary Laufer

The veterinarian never suggested that I give my cat a bath. It was my idea.

I was holding Mischief on the exam table when I noticed white flecks scattered on her black fur. "What's that?" I asked the vet.

"Just pieces of dried skin," he said. He had combed out some nasty mats in Mischief's hair, and now her sleek coat was covered with dandruff.

I felt a little guilty that I'd neglected to groom my cat, and I was eager to show the doctor what a good pet owner I really was. Without thinking, I blurted out, "Should I give her a bath?"

"A sponge bath might make her more comfortable," the vet said. "We sell a shampoo that would put some oils back into her skin."

I nodded as if I gave my cat baths all the time. When I

paid the bill, I asked the cashier to add on the shampoo the doctor recommended. She took a small bottle down from a shelf, and I saw the sticker. Fifteen dollars! The shampoo I bought for my own hair didn't cost that much.

Driving home, I recalled Mischief's one and only bath 10 years ago, right after she came to live with me. She'd picked up fleas at the animal shelter, and I tried to give her a flea bath in the tub. As soon as her paws touched the water, she panicked, climbing my bare arms like a tree and escaping through the open door. Over the years, she hated water so much that I used it as a deterrent, squirting her with the kitchen sprayer to keep her off the countertops.

I decided to do it in the half-bath downstairs, a tiny room with only a toilet and vanity. If Mischief got away from me this time, she couldn't go far. I knew the sound of running water would spook her, so before she was in the room, I filled three large plastic cups with warm water. I set the shampoo by the sink and hung a towel on the rack.

When everything was ready, I waited for Mischief to come to me. It would be a mistake to go to her. I'd just picked her up this morning to take her to the vet, and the grueling experience of having her mats untangled was undoubtedly still fresh in her memory. Coming into the bathroom had to be her idea, just as she willingly jumped into my lap whenever she wanted to be petted.

I left the door slightly ajar and looked out through the crack. Mischief's yellow eyes peeked at me from around the sofa. I stepped back behind the door, hoping to arouse her curiosity. After a minute, I looked again. She'd come out from the sofa and moved a little closer. She was so predictable.

When I checked a few seconds later, she was sitting just outside the door. She poked her nose into the bathroom as if to say, "What are you doing in here?" and padded through the doorway, first her head, next her middle and then her tail. When she was totally inside, I gently pushed on the door, easing it shut. She stiffened and turned around and meowed. She knew this was a trap!

I held out my arms to pick her up, but she scampered away and hid behind the toilet. I knelt down and pulled her out, stroked her until she purred and then set her on the vanity and quickly poured a little water on the area that had been matted. Her back arched and her claws clicked on the edge of the sink. She cried, she hissed, she flailed. I held her snugly so she couldn't scratch me, put a dab of the strong-smelling shampoo on the wet spot and worked it into a lather. She looked skinny with wet fur clinging to her ribs.

My plan had been to set Mischief in the sink and pour the cups of water over her, but I realized now that the faucet protruded too far into the sink bowl. She wouldn't fit! I didn't have a Plan B. Not knowing what else to do, I set the cat on the floor, backed out the door and shut it, leaving her meowing on the other side. Her pitiful cries reached my heart. I never should have attempted to give her a bath, but it was too late now.

On the bottle, it said to leave the shampoo on her fur for 10 minutes. That gave me time to figure out how I was going to catch the rinse water. I needed one of those oval plastic tubs that are made for bathing newborns. I went looking in closets for anything resembling a baby bathtub, found a bin filled with red and green Christmas bows and dumped them out.

One problem was solved, but another was waiting to happen. When I opened the bathroom door, Mischief squeezed out by my feet and ran as fast as a lightning bolt. The whole time I was gone, she must have been planning her getaway, just waiting for that door to open. I should have crawled in and blocked her with the bin. Now she was already upstairs, probably hiding under a bed.

With a sigh, I started up the steps, wondering if it was going to take me all afternoon to get Mischief back in the bathroom. But to my surprise, two little black ears stood out on the landing above. I slowly climbed the stairs and sat down on the step below her. "Poor kitty," I said. "I know you don't like to be wet. But we have to get that shampoo off you."

I reached up as if I were merely going to pet Mischief's head and instead, I grabbed her by the scruff of her neck. Her eyes grew round like full moons and her claws dug into the carpet for traction. I pried her off the carpet fibers and engulfed her in my arms.

Returning to the bathroom, I kicked the door shut, set the cat in the plastic bin and poured the clear water over her. The rinse water turned gray and bubbly as it ran off her fur and accumulated in the bottom of the tub. When it came in contact with her paws, Mischief lifted her shaking legs one at a time as if she were dancing. I poured the second cup of water on her and she scrambled to get out. "Let me finish," I said, holding down her rear end firmly and rinsing her with the stream of water from the third cup. "You're almost done."

I rubbed her with the towel and then bundled her up like a baby in a blanket. I had visions of drying her scraggly fur with my hair dryer, but as soon as I opened the door, she wiggled out of my arms, jumped down and took off, leaving me standing in the hallway with the empty towel and a sopping shirt.

A few minutes later, I found Mischief lying by the heating vent in the kitchen floor. When I bent down to give her some treats, she backed away and ran. It would be a long time before she'd trust me enough to sit in my lap again!

Mischief

Cat-aclysmic Curiosity

by
Janet Sheppard Kelleher

Never having had a cat in my home before 1975, I'm certain the scary event of that first momentous night is the reason I kept my distance for many years.

Shortly after graduating from college, I moved out of my childhood home into a small cottage on the other side of town. My first real freedom tasted like s'mores made with Godiva chocolate and sardines—which would teach anyone a lesson.

While applying for jobs, I decorated my little house with tie-dyed curtains and incense. My college roommate and I had been trying to get together since graduation, but I had been on the road with my summer job. Finally settled, I readied for a visit with my friend. The only problem—Lynn's cat, Hortense.

If Lynn came to South Carolina for a week, Hortense would, out of necessity, be my houseguest, as well. My landlord prohibited pets, but Horty wasn't *my* pet. I figured we could sneak him in since cats don't need to be walked. Who would be the wiser, right? My three-room cottage would be cramped, but certainly had more room than we ever shared in college, minus one cat.

So on the eve before my first day of real work after a fun summer job, Lynn arrived with Horty in tow. A huge, gorgeous, loving Siamese tomcat, he was obviously glad to see the end of an eight-hour trip.

After dinner, we made up the sofa bed in the living room and chatted till way too late. I enjoyed petting Horty for a while, stroking his soft furry coat. But he wouldn't let me stop. He kept nuzzling up under my hand. I didn't have to do anything much, just be there. He did most of the work, pushing his head first, then his arching back through the tunnel created by my cupped hand. He wanted more. I didn't. I wanted just to enjoy Lynn's company, not massage the cat after his hard day.

I didn't know how to stop petting him without offending Lynn or making her think that I didn't like Horty. I liked him fine. I just didn't realize I'd be enslaved as his personal masseuse!

Lynn finally corralled Hortense by settling down on the sofa bed with him curled by her side. Unfettered from the demands of this beautiful kitty, I fled to my room, closing the door behind me.

"Jan?!" Lynn called. "Remember, Horty needs access to the potty."

Crap! Literally! I fumed to myself. I swung open the

door. "You mean you didn't bring a litter box?"

"Horty doesn't use a litter box. He's trained to use the toilet."

"He's trained to use *your* toilet, Lynn. Not *my* toilet!" I shuddered, knowing full well this big guy would hold me captive again if he woke up and had to wee-wee—or worse—during the night. Tomorrow held a new adventure and I needed to sleep.

"Oh, all right," I said. I left the door cracked open just enough for Horty to meander his way to my bathroom.

First day jitters had me anticipating the worst with an all-male company. Sleep came slowly, but I must have been deep in the arms of Morpheus when a commotion scared the devil outta me.

Awakened by the sudden sound of nails on a chalkboard, I felt an octopus with claws fall onto my face. Scared witless, I swiftly flung the thing away from me. It catapulted into the wall adjacent to Lynn and she came running into the room.

Before my eyes had even focused, she cried, "Poor Horty. What have you done to him, Jan?!"

Still shaking from the scare like a holly in a high wind, I struggled to my senses.

"What have I done to him?!" I screamed. Lynn scooped up Horty, cradling him in his misery. "What about what he did to *me*?"

"Aw, he didn't hurt you."

"Well, he scared me into the middle of next week. That's something!"

Here's what we think happened. An oddly placed window

near the ceiling above the head of my bed called Horty's name. Apparently, he followed the beckon. Curiosity got the better of him. He leaped over me from the floor to get there. Only he missed the windowsill. His claws screeched down the wall in an attempt to grab onto something, landing him full force onto my face!

I don't know who scared whom the most, but I thought the Big Bad Wolf had me for sure! I've had a Palmetto bug crawl over my face in a motel room. I've had a mosquito the size of a hummingbird bite my face in the middle of the night while I camped out. But I've never had anything drop onto my face in my own bedroom, let alone a furry, prickly 15-pound bowling ball! I'm just grateful my bowling arm knew how to handle it.

Nearly 40 years have passed and I'm still a little nervous around cats. The feline species took up residence in our home when my best friend moved into our family's mother-in-law suite 12 years ago with Kitty Girl. I do think I prefer females. They tend to be more domesticated, less territorial and less demanding, which suits me just fine.

The thing I remember most, however, is the night curiosity nearly killed the cat, the cat's curiosity nearly killed me, and Lynn seemed to think I caused it all. I was concerned about that for a long time, so I'm glad cats have nine lives. I only knocked off one of Horty's; I wonder how many I have left.

The Killer Piano

by
Cliff Johnson

This is a story about cats, mice, rattlesnakes, a piano and sex. The setting is Folsom Prison—actually, on the grounds of Folsom Prison.

Our family consisted of mother, father, four children, two dogs and a cat named "Tashi." We lived in residence on the grounds for 17 years while I worked there. Known as "The Valley," about 35 homes made up the grounds and even though The Valley was located next to the prison, it was an ideal place to raise a family.

Our house was approximately 900 square feet and had a huge backyard. An open field of many acres extended beyond our fenced yard. The field was home to coyotes, possums, skunks, deer, rattlesnakes and, of course, mice. All of the above ended up on or near our yard with great frequency.

Tashi was Siamese. He lived in the house but had the run of the outdoors. A great hunter, Tashi sensed that since his family didn't know how to hunt, he would do it for us. Thus, he routinely left presents of dead critters on our doorstep. And because he had a knack for hunting, whenever Tashi meowed to be let back inside, we made sure he didn't have a surprise gift for us.

Our neighbors, who lived two houses down, also had a Siamese cat. They made the mistake of installing a cat door and their cat would take animals inside their house. On one occasion, the woman who lived there went to get a garment from her closet. When she opened the door, she was greeted by a live rattlesnake. She screamed so loud that everyone thought it was the prison's escape siren.

The Valley was a family-friendly neighborhood with frequent socializing. For those readers interested in the sex part—possibly kinky sex on the actual grounds of Folsom Prison—keep reading.

One evening, two of our next-door neighbors—a husband and wife—came over for drinks after work. We were in our living room enjoying appetizers and libations, some of which contained alcohol. Yes, we were having quite the little party.

It wasn't until we had consumed many beverages that I heard Tashi meow at the front door. I opened the door without giving it much thought, and Tashi entered with a mouse in his mouth.

Once Tashi was just inside the door, I realized he had brought another drinking buddy to the party. "No, Tashi! Go back outside! OUTSIDE!" I yelled.

That cat was always a good listener—he released the

mouse and went back outside, solo.

Our upright piano was located in the living room, right next to the front door. And, of course, that's where the mouse decided to hide—underneath the piano.

After many frantic screams by my wife and the female half of the visiting couple, I got a flashlight and asked the male half of the visiting couple to help me move the piano to look for the mouse. Both women were given the assignment of watching for the mouse in case it tried to escape from under the piano. Of course, they did this from a safe distance, both standing on the couch, never spilling a drop of their drinks.

We men rolled one end of the heavy piano out away from the wall to check in back. No mouse. We looked around the piano, in every direction. Still, no mouse.

"That's weird. It must have run someplace else," I said. Of course that made the women more upset. They downed their drinks.

Rolling the piano back into place, we were ready to start searching the rest of the house when my flashlight illuminated the front wheel of the piano. I couldn't believe my eyes—the wheel was lined with gray fur.

I started laughing, as did the other husband. The women, still standing on the couch, but now with empty glasses, thought I was drunk and was making up the story to get them to come down from the couch.

After considerable debate, and realizing they had empty glasses that wouldn't fill themselves, the women got down and viewed the wheel. Once they confirmed that it was, indeed, lined with mouse fur, they headed to the kitchen to pour refills for all of us. After a long and good round of laughter over the episode, the other husband said that it was the first time he had ever seen a mouse killed by a piano.

Author's note: The kinky sex part was excluded because of space limitations. It can be reported that it also involved the piano, but not the cat.

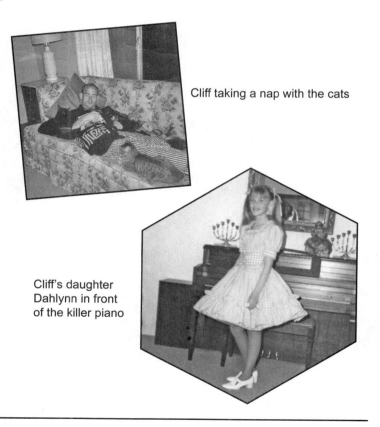

Cliff taking a nap with the cats

Cliff's daughter Dahlynn in front of the killer piano

The Stray-Cat Strut

The way felines dance right into our lives.

The Great One

by
Barbara Stretton

When he came to our deck five summers ago and looked at me with his George Clooney eyes, the romance began. He didn't come every day—only about once a week. I found out later he also visited other women.

He'd tried to win over the people across the street. They let him sleep on their back porch most of the summer, but they were afraid he'd terrorize their female cat Heidi, who got her name because she hid all the time. But they did give the handsome boy cat a name, "Moses," because they thought he was a wanderer.

Like his namesake, Moses wasn't a wanderer—he was a seeker.

That he sought out our deck shows how cunning he was. No doubt, he'd seen our other six cats looking out the window and he knew he could get to us.

Each time he came and I'd see those wonderful green

eyes looking at me from the railing of the deck—the noble gray face with its fine markings, the lean gray-striped body and long swishing tail—my heart would melt. I'd grab the nearest dish with leftover cat food and take it out, setting it in front of him as if he were royalty being served by a loyal servant. I dubbed him "Guest Cat."

After putting the food down on the deck, I'd go back inside and watch from the window as he ate. He'd lick the plate clean, glance at me once more with those wonderful eyes, and then stride across the deck and take off through the backyard.

One day as I was getting in my car to go to the gym, our neighbor came over. "We took Moses to the shelter," she said. "They're having an adoption day this weekend, so we thought he might find a home."

Thoughts raced through my brain: *What? No more George Clooney eyes looking at me from the deck? No more noble markings to admire? No more bestowing food on him and watching him enjoy it?*

As I took my shower at the gym after my workout, I felt the tears coming. I let them flow as the water of the shower poured over me. After I got dressed, I took out my little journal and wrote, "Guest Cat is gone." When I got home, I told my husband about it, as tears continued to wet my cheeks.

A day or so later, my husband came home and said, "Let's go get him."

We drove to the animal shelter in Stamford. There he was in a wire cage in the back room at the shelter. When he saw us, he turned his head upside down and rolled over.

"Take me, take me," he said, not knowing he had already won us over.

We had to fill out a form and give two references that showed we were the right people to have a cat. They even called our vet to be sure we were responsible owners. I liked that they did that. It showed they didn't let cats go to just anyone who walked in. We paid $50 for him, a cat we could have picked up from our deck for free. But the money included his neutering operation and his rabies shot, a requirement in Connecticut. So he was really a bargain.

We didn't get to take him home right then and there. He was sent to a vet for his operation and we picked him up about a week later. Meantime, we puzzled over what name to give him. We didn't want to call him Moses. We went down to the library and looked at Rudyard Kipling stories about tigers, but since in those stories the tiger usually ended up as a hearth rug, we rejected that. He came home without a name—still "Guest Cat."

The next morning, our newest family member presented us with a list of demands. No more leftover cat food. If he got that or anything he didn't want, he'd performed an elaborate routine. He'd lift a paw and swipe it across the dish as if covering it with cat litter. Then he'd do the same with the other paw. And just for good measure, he'd turn and do it again with both paws. I realized it had to be Fancy Feast or nothing and only Fancy Feast Whitefish and Tuna. And not even that on some days.

I watched him making himself at home. He walked across the floor of the living room with a John Wayne swagger, and then sat on the back of the couch to watch chipmunks in the hedge. His fine markings shone in the sun, and that's when a name came to me, the name of the king of Egypt who had sent Moses into the desert to begin his long search—Ramses. It fit his noble profile with the fine markings, like an Egyptian painting. And even more, it fit his noble attitude. But my husband has always named the boy cats, so I didn't share my idea with him.

One night, as we were finishing dinner on our deck, my husband said, "We could always call him Ramses."

I fully expected Rod Serling to step out of the shadows and the music from *The Twilight Zone* to begin playing. The answer was, of course, that Ramses had whispered his real name in our ears while we slept.

What a fitting name it turned out to be, and not just because of his royal bearing. He'd race around the house, jumping from the chair to the mantel, from the bed to the top of the TV, chasing balls and the other cats. So he got plenty of ram-related nicknames, such as "Rambo" and "Mr. Rambunctious." But most often, we would say in a loud, deep voice, like the announcer on the truck commercial, "RAM!"

Now, when he looks up at me with those wonderful eyes from his dish of Fancy Feast, I know he is, indeed, Ramses the Great.

A Matching Set

by
Shannon Brown

I could tell something was awry when I tried to let my cat Oreo out for the night. She didn't get very far into the backyard. Instead, she took a few steps, stopped and started meowing into the darkness. I was worried there might be a raccoon outside, so I stepped out, hoping to scare it away. But whomever Oreo was talking to didn't budge. Oreo sat fixed in place and continued to meow, and then I heard something meow back.

As my eyes adjusted to the darkness, I saw a cat sitting there. I recognized her. She had been to my door before, and I had mistaken her for Oreo. From both the side and behind, the two cats were nearly identical—black fur, black tails, white paws and white underbellies.

You could only tell the difference between them when you looked at them dead on. Their faces were different— the new cat had a patch of white just below her nose, while Oreo had a streak of white on her chin and above her nose. The other cat was smaller than Oreo, too, so much smaller that I started calling her "Oreo Junior," and then "Minnie," short for "Miniature Oreo."

The little cat looked at me, but made no motion to leave the yard. *She must be a neighbor's cat,* I thought, noticing she was wearing a collar. The collar didn't have identity tags on it, only a bell. The collar was also sitting on her at an angle. *Is this some sort of new style?* No, it didn't seem right. I bent down and saw that the collar had slipped behind her leg somehow. I gingerly pulled out her leg and let the collar return to its normal position. It hung too loosely on her, so I pulled it off and noticed the leather part was broken, and the lining underneath had lost its elasticity.

I decided to take the collar inside, and as I opened the door slightly, Minnie invited herself in with a series of meows. *Meow, meow, meow,* she kept chatting away, until she reached the kitchen. Destination: Oreo's bowl. I intended to pour her a separate bowl and set it outside, but the little cat had other ideas. She started devouring the remaining food in Oreo's bowl with an untamed furor. When she was done, Minnie looked up and began meowing again.

Like most humans, I am not fluent in the language of meow, but I think I understood what Minnie was saying. Each meow was a sentence. "Thank you for getting rid of that horrid collar digging into my fur," was one sentence, and, "Please feed me now," was another. Her most vocal meow was a statement—"This is my home, why don't you understand? I'm home."

Minnie stared at me, tossing pitiful daggers with her eyes. I got her a fresh bowl of food and took it outside. As soon as Minnie went out, Oreo came in. Because of our rental agreement, Oreo can't be strictly an indoor cat, so she was outside a lot.

Picking up Oreo to put her back outside, Minnie ran back inside. When I finally rounded her up and returned her to the back porch, Oreo casually ambled back inside. I eventually grew tired of constant cat wrangling, so I let Oreo out through a different door and did my best to ignore the small new face now keeping a vigil at the closed back door.

I wondered why Oreo, the more dominant of the two, hadn't chased off the new cat. Oreo was larger and knew how to manage on her own. She, too, had also just shown up one day, like Minnie. I suspected she was a foreclosure cat, left behind when the people around the corner moved. Their house emptied in the course of a night, without the usual fanfare. No open houses, coming-soon signs or major-company moving vans— the place was occupied one day and empty the next.

I thought Minnie would have found her way home that night, but she was at the door in the morning and more than happy to receive the bowl I laid out. She wasn't skin and bones, but appeared healthy and had very soft and silky fur, though she ate like there was no tomorrow. I wondered if this was because of the bell on her collar. The poor thing probably scared off any potential prey.

I have plenty of friends who didn't understand why I was feeding the new kitty. They had pat sayings lined up. "You know, once you start feeding a cat they'll never leave," or "They probably have a bowl lined up at the back door of every house on the block." I ignored them—I couldn't let an innocent and obviously distressed creature starve.

The next day, I put up flyers all over town, and I looked for "missing cat" postings, as well. No one called, and Minnie made herself at home. As soon as the door would open, she would come in like a shot and head straight to her bowl, emptying it quickly, then she would move on to finish up Oreo's bowl.

Even when I made it clear that there would be more food available, Minnie would devour it. I was worried she was pregnant. I later discovered not only was she not pregnant, but she was not a girl at all! Minnie's name was converted to "Mini," still short for Miniature, though he didn't stay miniature for very long.

I thought Mini was a really small cat, but turns out he was just a teenage boy with a typical teen appetite. He grew into a beautiful, regular-sized fellow with silky fur and a love of cuddling. He'll sit on your lap for hours, purring and kneading. He even lets me pet his belly, unlike the average cat, his way thanking me for taking him in. I guess Mini suspected all along that I was a big softy, destined to have a matching set.

Mini (left) and Oreo

Luigi

by
Michele Cemo

One evening, as I got out of my car and began the trek through the expansive, well-lit landscaping toward my apartment building, I felt the presence of someone behind me. The odd thing was that I hadn't seen anyone or heard any footsteps.

I was scared, but my fear forced me to look. I had to know what was behind me! When I did, I found a large black cat following me.

Relieved that my stalker was a feline, I gave it a few pets and continued on to my apartment. The cat followed me to my door then followed me right inside, like it had lived there all its life. Since my apartment complex had a strict "no-pet" policy, I guessed it was a stranger to our neighborhood. But the cat certainly felt entitled to come into my home.

Once inside, I realized that "it" was a "he." I gave my guest some lunchmeat, enjoyed his company for a short while then set him outside. He was very calm and friendly, had lovely green eyes, but wasn't too talkative. Before he headed to parts unknown, the cat looked at me as if to say, "Thank you."

I didn't see him for a few days. Then one evening, he appeared again on the pathway to my apartment. We repeated the routine from our first meeting, and again I did not see him for a few days. He was a healthy-looking animal, appeared well fed and wasn't road-worn or flea-bitten. I just assumed he was a beloved pet who liked to roam and enjoy the hospitality of others.

As time went on, he appeared more often, and I found myself calling him "Luigi." I'm not sure why I chose that name, but he did like salami and provolone. He also had a good appetite and winning personality. So the name fit.

Over time, I made Luigi my unofficial cat. I asked my neighbors about him, and although several people who had seen him hanging around admitted to giving him a tidbit or two, there was no consensus on how long he had been there or where he had come from.

During that time, I was single. It was just Luigi and me. But about two years after Luigi came into my life, I met the man I later married. After we had tied the knot, we bought a home and Luigi became our official adoptee.

That's when the real fun began. As a cat with the run of the household and the yard, Luigi came into his own. Even though he loved his cat food, he loved "people food" even more.

True to his Italian name, Luigi had an insatiable appetite. I found him checking out the kitchen counters and our lunch bags for tidbits. He even enjoyed staring into an open refrigerator. Anywhere food was a possibility, you would find Luigi.

Finally having a nice kitchen to cook in—and a husband and cat who loved to eat—my French and Italian roots took hold. I adored cooking and had an innate love of baking. Considering Luigi's obsession with food, our cat had chosen the perfect family.

Sometimes Luigi's food-lust became problematic, such as the time I made a chocolate cake. I set the cake layers on the counter to cool and found them later with little bites out of them. Chocolate can make felines ill, but Luigi was perfectly fine and seemed quite happy with himself.

No food was below Luigi's notice. I loved roasting seeds and nuts to snack on, and one day, I roasted a few cups of sunflower seeds. I set them on the counter to cool, only to find a completely empty pan when I went back into the kitchen to put the treat into my lunch bag.

For our first Thanksgiving as a family—and it was a holiday meal I had never cooked before—Luigi became fascinated with the turkey. I cooked the giblets for him as his Thanksgiving treat, and my husband and I were careful to protect the turkey during our meal.

After dinner, we picked the carcass clean, saving the meat for leftovers. In a blink of an eye, the carcass disappeared, and we didn't find it until spring. While cleaning up the backyard from a long winter, we came upon Luigi's stash while trimming back overgrown bushes. It truly was a treasure trove of delights only a feline could love—a rotting turkey carcass, remnants of birds and a few pieces of trash that had contained food. Yes, Luigi was a food hoarder.

Luigi continued his love of food for many years. When I first took him in, the vet said he was about four years old. Well, Luigi lived with us for another 16 years. And during that time, we had two daughters. Luigi treasured the girls, especially during meal times when they would drop food from their highchairs!

We have had many cats since, some very sweet, some sassy and all unique. But not one could hold a candle to Luigi and his love of life and food and family.

Luigi

The Odd Couple

by

Marsha Porter

One summer, a gray tomcat with white paws and face markings settled in to the small garden patch that ran along-side my garage. Each morning, he would lie on the ledge beneath the garage window, soaking up the sun's early rays.

Although he wouldn't let me pet him, he gladly accepted the food and water I put out for him. Everyone assumed he was my cat since he was always in front of my house.

He had a muscular barrel-chested body, which made his legs appear proportionately too short. Rather than walk, he seemed to swagger. As he seemed to be the king of the jungle—a term I used to refer to my neighborhood—I began calling him "Lion."

He appeared to be a tough guy with a neck that vanished into his shoulders. A friend of mine hinted that he was probably getting into a lot of fights and on his peaceful nights, siring far too many offspring. "You should have him neutered," she ominously advised.

As before, he would not let me catch him, so I rented a humane trap. Instead of catching Lion, I found a possum in the cage on my first morning out. The possum, true to its reputation, played dead, refusing to leave when I opened the cage. Finally, using a hanger, I lifted the cage until the possum reluctantly tumbled out and dashed toward the bushes.

Lion resisted entering the cage for his regular cat food. It took a can of albacore tuna to entice him. When he finally took the bait, he glared at me from behind the cage bars. Undeterred by his obvious displeasure, I proudly took him to a nearby vet for the procedure and shots. After charging me $138, the vet callously suggested I not get attached to him. She said he was a street cat—too tough to be domesticated and not worth the effort. I was incensed and baffled by my vet's inability to see what a treasure Lion really was.

I returned him to his little garden and continued feeding him. Occasionally, he would allow me to lightly stroke his head while he ate, but he still refused to be held.

About that time, Lion was joined by a companion, one that was heard long before he was seen. Sometimes, as Lion lay calmly and majestically on his ledge, a mournful wail would come from inside the dense bushes below. Thinking an injured animal was crying out for help, I'd try to peer in at it, but all I could glimpse was a dirty cream-colored thing slinking further back out of view.

I decided to watch for this stranger from my kitchen window during Lion's feeding time. Lion would eat his fill, and then stroll over to the lawn. Soon after, a Siamese-looking cat darted out and devoured the meal's remains, always managing to disappear before I could open the door.

This strange couple continued its relationship for some weeks before the Siamese, which I called "Whinetta" in honor of his pitiful cries, ventured out more boldly. I began to put out two plates and the two soon ate side by side. Whinetta eventually occupied the ledge in calm repose, along with his mentor, which made me feel especially proud when I walked past them.

Whinetta became quite tame and welcomed my pats. Without the drama of capturing him in a humane trap, he was shortly off to a new vet to be neutered.

Around Halloween, Lion showed up with one eye swollen shut. I tried to capture him for treatment, but he ran off every time I approached. Naturally, I returned to the humane trap since it had worked before. No dice! Lion remembered what had happened the last time he went in that thing, and he wasn't about to be fooled again.

Days passed and Lion's shut eye bulged and watered. I had to get him! The vet gave me some kitty tranquilizers to put in his food. He ate heartily and appeared ready to fall asleep, but each time I tried to pick him up, he ran. Two hours later and with the help of a friend, I had him. Actually, I lured him with more food, first on the porch then on the threshold of my house. Right at my door, he slumped, finally succumbing to the relaxers.

We rushed Lion to the emergency vet clinic. When the vet pulled Lion's swollen eyelid back, I was distressed to see the bloody pulp that should have been his eye.

"There's a foxtail in there," was the efficient vet's prognosis. "It's been there a while, working its way through the eye. May not be able to save his sight," he concluded.

I was crying, imagining how painful this must have been for Lion. The doctor quickly removed the foxtail and sent me home with some eye ointment. "You'll have to give it four times a day, and then we'll see if he has any vision left in that eye."

I agreed to the treatment but immediately panicked, realizing Lion wouldn't want me to handle him. That's when I decided it didn't matter what he wanted—I would do what was best for him and hope he didn't scratch my eyes out for doing so.

As it turned out, it wasn't half-bad. I kept Lion in a large cage in my garage so I wouldn't have to chase him. The ointment must have felt soothing to him because after the first application, he stopped fighting me. I took advantage of his new-found dependence on me by cuddling and petting him as much as he'd allow. A week later, his eye was open, no longer a bloody mess. The vet instructed me to continue with the ointment for 10 more days, which I gladly did. Miraculously, the foxtail left a scar just above his retina and didn't impair his vision at all.

Throughout all this, Whinetta continued to be fed, rubbing up against my leg as I put his food down. From the garage window ledge, he'd peer into the garage to check on Lion. Occasionally, he'd let out his trademark wail just to let Lion know he was there for him.

It was now mid-November and near freezing. I let Whinetta stay in the garage with Lion. They adjusted well, cuddling up on the comforter I'd given them.

At last, they were tame enough to move into the house. They now share the back bedroom and, to this day, continue to be the best of friends, wrapping themselves around each other whenever the temperature drops.

Who would have guessed that a tough guy like Lion would share his food with a shrinking violet—or should I say shrinking Vince—like Whinetta? Who'd have imagined the secretive Whinetta bravely standing guard on Lion's ledge while he recovered? The friendship that had blossomed between this odd couple brought out the best in each of them.

Whinetta

Lion

Guardian Angel

by
Julie Royce

The first nerve-wracking week of my new job had ended at six that Friday night, and I had survived. I trudged across a cobblestone street and down the plank sidewalks of Old Sacramento toward the parking ramp. Strangers stood along the way, pointing. Set against a stormy sky mottled with brilliant blue patches streaked a double rainbow—the first I'd ever seen. I looked for no meaning or sign in the splendor of its arced symmetry—not then, at least. It seemed enough to glimpse nature's artistry after a wearing week.

During a six-month period, my life had become a how-to guide on punishing oneself with stress. I struggled with after-effects of failed eye surgery. I had retired from my position as an Assistant Attorney General with the State of Michigan and had accepted a job in private practice with the largest workers' compensation law firm in California. Those situations alone justified jitters.

Because we were cautious, my husband, Bob, and I devised a responsible plan: We sold the home we had built together. He moved into an apartment and continued working in Lansing after I made the cross-country move. We'd ensure my new position agreed with me before he quit his job and joined me.

Two weeks before I departed for Sacramento, my father suffered a heart attack and refused bypass surgery. The most favorable prognosis gave him months to live. "I'll be home for a visit next summer," I said. I kissed him goodbye, wearing a stoic mask that dissolved into tears as I drove away. I would return home, but my heart told me he would be gone.

The apartment I rented in Sacramento had three bedrooms. I furnished it with a twin box spring and mattress, not even a bed frame. The extra bedrooms would act as storage when Bob arrived with our furniture. The emptiness did little to allay the crippling pangs of isolation. I splurged on a 12-inch color TV to mitigate the unrelenting silence.

I was strong and resilient, but I was alone.

The new job had one saving virtue—I worked 12-hour days that left little time to think about a life that seemed as barren as my living quarters. Leave work, drive home, turn on the evening news, pop a Lean Cuisine into the microwave, eat it with a plastic fork I'd saved from Jack in the Box. When the news ended, I read statutes and California case law until I could no longer keep my eyes open. The next day, I repeated the cycle.

The second Monday after my move, a surprise waited for me when I got home. Halfway up the flight of stairs to my apartment's landing lounged a gray cat basking in the day's final glimmer of sunshine. I paused before climbing closer, hoping my new friend would stay awhile, but he gave me wide berth and started down the steps. Midway, he paused and stared back, his yellow-green eyes seeming to ask, "Promise you won't give me a kick or swat me with a broom?" He had the caution of an abandoned cat, but his glossy, well-groomed coat told a different story. No protruding ribs or burrs, no scratches or scars, marked him a stray.

I unbolted my apartment door and let it gape wide as I headed to the kitchen, opened a can of tuna and dumped half of it into the palm of my right hand.

Walking back to the porch, I thought of a proverb my mother had shared when I was a little girl and we had taken in a stray cat—"You will always be lucky if you know how to make friends with strange cats." My new life was immersed in challenges and I craved a dose of good fortune.

"It's OK, Smoky." I didn't know what his name had been in other lives, but at that moment he became Smoky to me. I concluded from his size and attitude he was male. If my assumption was wrong, it had no impact on our relationship. "I come in peace and with offerings," I purred. My visitor remained on the second step from the top and came no closer. I dumped the tuna from my hand to the concrete landing and backed away.

He may have had reservations, but he was also hungry. He crept near enough to eat, but between bites, he shot suspicious glances my way. He licked a paw and washed it over his face before he loped back downstairs and skittered away. "That's OK," I called after him. "I'll accept your rules. I hope you come back to see me again."

The next evening, he waited on my landing, crouched against the building so I could pass without invading his comfort zone. Again, I unlocked the apartment door and left it ajar. I retrieved the other half of the tuna I'd opened the previous night and poured a saucer of milk. I set the feast down, and then plopped cross-legged on the porch with little concern that I'd ruin my best linen slacks.

I gave Smoky space, but I refused to go inside. He eyed me and my gifts. After several seconds, he ended the stand-off and covered the distance between him and the food. A day later, he gobbled the Fancy Feast I'd bought to bribe him, but instead of scampering away, he remained to have his head scratched.

By the second week of our meetings, Smoky had zeroed in on my schedule and also met me at the door as I left at 6 A.M. From then on, as soon as the alarm went off, I hurried to the front porch to find him waiting to help me greet the day. I'd invite him to hang out as I showered and got ready for work. As inducement to return, I provided a couple of kitty treats before we exited the apartment—me for my law office, and him for wherever he spent his time away from me. Down the steps he'd disappear, to other missions or other people.

Smoky and I enjoyed a steady relationship. I counted on him to be there when I got home, an antidote to feeling sorry for myself. He never stood me up. He explored each corner and crevice and cubbyhole of the apartment with movements of grace and agility, his own version of ballet. He became the art and soul of my stark retreat until my husband arrived with furniture months later.

During our time together, Smoky buoyed my spirits more than a Chihuly sculpture or a Monet painting, and his purr calmed me like Mozart and Bach. He was my escape from daily hassle. I sat on my bed, back against the hard wall, a book on my legs. He'd prance over, tip his head up toward mine and, in a meow that was unmistakable, tell me to put aside the reading material for a few minutes so he could curl up on my lap. I would prop the books on a pillow at my side and stroke his velvety fur as I read. With Smoky's company, tension drained.

I never owned Smoky. Maybe no one ever owns a cat, but I had niggling suspicions that I shared his presence with someone else. On one particularly cold night, I was tempted to let Smoky stay inside, but I worried that if he had a home, his owners would be frantic. As a compromise, I taped a box closed, cut out a Smoky-sized opening, stuffed one of my two blankets inside and placed the finished project on the porch. I threw in a few kitty treats and hoped he'd be warm enough. At midnight, before I went to bed, I checked, but Smoky was gone. If he shared his time with other humans, there was also something about me that made him return with the regularity of the afternoon traffic jam on my commute.

Work remained stressful and Smoky continued his visits even after Bob arrived. Three months later, my husband and I found the perfect house and I began worrying about Smoky. I wondered if he had a family. I wanted to take him with us, but I didn't want to steal someone's cat.

The movers were scheduled for Saturday morning. I started canvasing the apartment complex to see if anyone knew who owned my cat. If no one claimed him, he was mine. I went to the rental office and asked for a list of all renters with cats. The search proved futile. Friday night before the move, I came home, but Smoky wasn't there to greet me. He wasn't there Saturday morning, either.

The joy of a new house and getting settled couldn't squelch my nagging worry that Smoky had met with harm, and that, in some way, I'd let him down. Many nights, I stopped at the apartment complex on my way home from work, but I never saw him again.

A month after we moved, an article appeared in *The Sacramento Bee* with a picture that was either Smoky or his doppelganger. I choose to believe it was Smoky, and that he had a family. His people had moved from Seattle to Sacramento. At a rest stop along the way, their cat had jumped from the car and was left behind. Six months later, the cat had tracked them down and showed up on their doorstep. I think Smoky always intended to find his humans, but detoured long enough to play my guardian angel.

Smoky

The Big Show

by
Stacey Gustafson

For thousands of years, man's best friend has been the dog. But what happens when dog's best friend is a cat?

Growing up in the Midwest, I tended to the usual menagerie of pets-gone-wrong—goldfish left in the sun, gerbils trapped in heating vents and hamsters lost in the grass. I proved to be a complete failure at pet ownership, yet my parents rewarded me with a dog. Go figure.

One snowy night in December, a muffled *meow* emanated from our front porch. Mom cracked open the storm door, and a subzero blast of icy wind pushed her backward. She held the door open with her hip, glanced down and spied a tiny mixed Tabby cat with faint brown and black stripes covering her body. The cat scratched at the door and tilted her head as if to say, "Please, may I come in?"

Our six-month-old mixed-breed puppy, Tippy, named

for his black fur and white paws, released a high-pitched bark and turned in circles just inside the front door.

"Shhhh, be quiet," I said to Tippy, patting his head.

"Poor thing," said my mother, a sucker for homeless pets. "Must be freezing."

"If you let her in, she'll never leave," I said, with teenage authority.

By this time, Tippy had worked himself into a foaming frenzy and shoved his face through my mother's legs to get a better look at the cat outside.

Giving in, my mother opened the door a bit more. Wasting no time, that Tabby cat strutted into the living room and pounced on our reclining chair. It commandeered a comfy place on the headrest and stared down at us, as if to say, "Now what are you going to do about it?"

"Why don't you make yourself at home?" I said to the cat.

From that moment on, Tippy and Ms. Kitty—her new name—napped together on the recliner, the cat balanced on the headrest and the dog curled up in a ball on the chair's cushion.

Those two became the best of friends. Whenever Tippy nudged Ms. Kitty with his nose and whipped his tail like a propeller, it signaled that playtime was on! They would tear out of the room, and Ms. Kitty would jump over Tippy's back. She would taunt him then skid under the bed, out of reach. Ms. Kitty was the one to decide when the fun was over by dive-bombing back to her spot on the chair.

The neighbors were aware of our pets' antics. Many times, they would holler from over the fence as they barbecued, "Bring out the dog and cat!" they said, wanting a dinner show.

Let the games begin! And they did. Upon hearing their request, we would fling open the door, just like the parting of curtains at Ringling Brothers Circus. The crowd cheered as Tippy pursued Ms. Kitty, the two dashing helter-skelter throughout the backyard. Next, Ms. Kitty would roll into a ball and freeze in place, letting Tippy drag her around by the scruff of her neck. Then Tippy would toss Ms. Kitty like a baton across the lawn. Believe it or not, Ms. Kitty loved this and would race back to Tippy for a second act.

For the finale, Ms. Kitty would leapfrog over Tippy, just like famed gymnast Nadia Comaneci did in the Olympics. Back and forth Ms. Kitty flew, placing her front paws on Tippy's back as if he were a pommel horse. When Ms. Kitty did her amazing dismount, the crowd hollered, "Do it again! Do it again!"

A few months later, I noticed Ms. Kitty moving at a slower pace. She refused to budge from her perch on the recliner, even when Tippy did his best to egg her on.

"Mom, does she look a little fat?" I asked, bending closer to examine the cat.

"Yes. Ms. Kitty is soon to be a Misses," replied Mom.

One morning, Tippy howled at the top of the basement steps, begging us to follow him downstairs. Ms. Kitty was nestled in a cardboard box on top of the washing machine, surrounded by her four kittens, ranging in color from solid orange to striped gray. From that point forward, Tippy took up dog patrol at the base of the washing machine, overprotective of his pal and her kittens. If our friends leaned in too close, Tippy would let out a low growl—"Look, but don't touch."

After we found new owners for the kittens, Ms. Kitty disappeared. Tippy waited for her at the front door for weeks, but she never returned. Ms. Kitty left us the same way she came into our life, suddenly and with aplomb.

Stacey and Ms. Kitty (Stacey shared that
her mom wasn't the greatest photographer)

Soundtrack of Love

by
Rosie Sorenson

There's a new soundtrack to our lives. Sometimes my husband, Steve, and I hear a "B-flat," sometimes an "A," sometimes a trill. With each note, we're reminded that every cat snores to her own drummer. You heard right—Sweetie Pie snores. Who knew?

Prior to bringing her into our Northern California home, Sweetie Pie lived for 15 years in Buster Hollow with a colony of homeless kitties I've mom-catted for 17 years. She was, and still is, the funniest cat around.

Sweetie Pie is small. Even now, she looks to be the size of a nine-month-old kitten. She had a litter of two before I could catch and spay her. One of her kittens was disabled, impossible to catch and disappeared within two weeks of the first sighting. The other gray-striped baby—Sonny Gray— was her doppelganger, only larger in size with eyes a little less amber-colored.

Sweetie Pie rebuffed Sonny Gray's overtures of friendship time and again, issuing her all-purpose hiss whenever he drew near. She either did not recognize her own flesh and blood or was put out that she'd been forced, against her will, into early motherhood. *Why wasn't I consulted?* she must have wondered. No one stepped up to claim paternity.

It took me two years to develop a relationship with Sweetie Pie. After that, she was my darlin', rushing out to greet me every day when I came to feed the colony. Thirteen years ago, Sweetie Pie developed a mad crush on my then new sweetheart, Steve, when he joined me on my rounds. I wouldn't exactly say my feelings were hurt, but geez. I'd been out there every day—rain or shine—courting her, loving her, petting her, feeding her, and now? Steve was her savior? Puh-leeze! Fickle felines.

You'd have to see it to believe it, but whenever Steve accompanied me, Sweetie Pie would rush down the path toward us, crying, "Eeee, Eeee." Upon getting closer, she would collapse into the brown paper bag of food sitting near Steve's feet. "Omigod, Omigod, Omigod," she seemed to cry. "My man's here, my man's here!" She didn't know whether to eat, get more pets or hiss at a neighboring cat's butt, such was her excitement. She danced on her tippy-toes for Steve, rubbing against his legs and flopping her head into his hands, all the while smiling.

This went on for 13 years, until July. Prior to July, there was the occasional injury in the colony—a limping cat here, an abscessed cat there, a runny cat eye requiring the attention of a vet. But nothing prepared me for July.

One cat after another turned up injured, six in all, the wounds appearing on the left side of their bodies. As injuries go, they were rather minor and consisted of a superficial scrape or two along the left flank inflicted by some unknown critter. *Is the perp another cat? A skunk? A raccoon?* I wondered. Neither Steve nor I had any idea.

The only clue we had was that one day Steve saw the longhaired black cat—Barry—attack Sweetie Pie as she emerged from her home in the blackberry bushes near the path. She was heading down to visit Steve on a day when I couldn't go. The following afternoon, I noticed a new scrape on her side. I blamed Barry.

Barry had joined the colony eight months earlier, origin unknown. The other cats gave him a wide berth. He never came close enough for me to socialize him, let alone confirm his sex, but I was pretty sure he was male.

After her injury, we trapped Sweetie Pie and took her to the vet, who was just as puzzled by the nature of the wound. The vet couldn't figure out how it had been inflicted, noting that if it were a raccoon or skunk who attacked, the cat would have been eviscerated. Same for a dog. Another cat? Possible, but how?

We might never know, but I couldn't risk Sweetie Pie's life by returning her to the colony, not until we trapped Barry and found him another home.

Notice how I said that so casually: ". . . not until we trapped Barry . . ." You don't know the meaning of FRUSTRATION until you've tried to trap a homeless cat. I rounded up the best trappers I could find. We each, in turns, spent

HOURS trying to coax him into the trap. "Ha-ha!" Barry seemed to say each time he walked around the trap and stood on top of it, refusing to go inside. Well, that's not exactly true. He did go into one trap and stepped on the metal plate, but before it closed—and we're talking nanoseconds—he got his butt right back out. We finally gave up.

It's a good set of cat-loving friends who will foster a cat such as Sweetie Pie. David and Deborah opened their hearts and home to her, and for three months, I hoped and prayed she would settle in and become "their kitty." She did not. No fault of theirs. The only time she perked up was when Steve and I came to visit her. Then, she'd come out of the closet and dance around with joy. "My people are here!" she said with her eyes when she saw us. She made it clear that she was stubbornly unadoptable.

During those three months, not another cat was injured, even though Barry was still present at Buster Hollow. Steve and I realized that we may have unfairly accused Barry of the attacks, and that maybe Sweetie Pie would be just fine if we returned her to her outdoor home. After all, she'd done well for 15 years.

Once we made the decision, we headed out to pick her up and return her, that is, until we actually saw her again. Her yelps and purrs, her happiness to see us broke our hearts.

On the way home, with the pet taxi in the back seat, I said to Steve, "Well, why don't we just keep her overnight, then take her to the vet for more tests tomorrow, to make sure she's healthy enough to live on her own again. After that, we can take her back out there."

We did, and she was, and we couldn't. She'd worked her magic on us. We. Just. Couldn't. Let. Her. Go.

This is how we've come to find out that she snores. We'd never been privy to Sweetie Pie's nighttime routine when she lived outdoors, so we didn't know.

Which brings me to ask, if a cat snores in the forest and there's no one around to hear it, does she make a sound?

Well, now there's someone around to hear it. In fact, two someones, serenaded every night by the soft trills of her love.

Sweetie Pie

Best Friends Come in All Sizes

by

Steve Liddick

It was raining when I returned from the barn to feed our horses and noticed a bedraggled cat on the porch of our Pennsylvania farmhouse. He was attacking a bowl of cat food as though he had not eaten in a while.

"What are you doing out here, Tiger?" I asked. This was odd, because Tiger was strictly an indoor cat.

"Not Tiger," my wife, Sherry, said from the doorway. "He just wandered in and I put some food out for him."

No surprise. All five of our cats had "just wandered in." With so many of them out there needing a good home, the idea of buying a cat was an alien concept.

We had a large fenced-in compound alongside the house and an entry flap for the felines to come and go as they pleased. That way, they were indoor/not-quite-outdoor cats, safe from roaming wild critters.

Sherry named the new boy "T.C.," for Top Cat. From the beginning, he was an indoor/outdoor cat. During the day, T.C. would hang out with our horses in the barnyard. He became friends with a palomino named Dusty who didn't seem to like anyone, human or equine. And for good reason—no one had ever treated Dusty humanely before we got her, and she never entirely trusted that we would not hurt or neglect her, either.

But Dusty truly loved T.C. They often went nose to nose in affectionate greeting. It was common to see T.C. walking among Dusty's enormous hooves without a care that the half-ton animal could squash him flat.

When evening came, I would go up to the barnyard, pick up T.C. and wear him like a fur piece around my neck as we walked back to the house for the night. From then on and for the rest of the time we lived in Pennsylvania, T.C. remained an indoor/outdoor cat.

Over time, T.C. became my cat and I became his human. We were inseparable. If I sat down, he was in my lap. If I got up from my chair to go to the kitchen, T.C. was close behind. I often referred to him as the son I never had. And T.C. showed his gratitude for being rescued by occasionally putting a dead vole or field mouse in Sherry's barn boots. Looking at it from a cat's perspective, those were generous gifts.

Eventually, we moved back to California for my job, with the cats in separate carriers on the plane and the horses trucked across the country in a stock trailer.

For the dozen final years of my nearly half-century career as a radio newscaster, I was a correspondent for a network that provided Sacramento regional news for distribution to affiliated northern California radio stations. I worked out of my home sound studio.

T.C. helped. Trying to write newscasts with a cat sitting on your lap with his paws sometimes touching the keyboard is not the most efficient arrangement, I'll admit.

As I was working one morning, I heard an odd sound coming from my computer.

Dee-dee-dee-dee.

At first, I couldn't figure out what was causing it.

Dee-dee-dee-dee.

Then I noticed that while T.C. was standing with his back feet on my lap and his front feet on the desk in front of the keyboard, he was drooling onto the keys. Apparently, the moisture shorted out something.

Since I was on deadline, as one always is in the radio business, I was in a panic. I was only halfway finished writing my news and I suddenly had no word-processor capabilities. Then I remembered that I had another keyboard. I hauled it out from the "things-that-are-too-good-to-throw-away-because-I-might-use-them-sometime" pile. I hooked it up, the noise stopped and I was able to continue.

Well, as much as I enjoyed T.C.'s company while I worked, I couldn't risk those kinds of delays again. So I put a pad on a table beside my workspace. That became his perch and he could look down at me while I worked. Occasionally, he would reach out with a paw to touch my arm.

Years later, I'd had major surgery and was in the hospital for four days. When I got home, I was in pain and bedridden. T.C. was there to greet me. He raced around the living room when I arrived. I struggled to get into bed. He huddled down beside me, wrapped both paws around my forearm and stayed that way for hours.

I had never felt so welcomed home in my life.

Nowhere is it written that a person's best friend has to be another human . . . or even a dog. Mine is a cat. T.C., to be exact.

T.C. and Steve

NYMB Series Founders

Together, Dahlynn and Ken McKowen have 60-plus years of professional writing, editing, publication, marketing and public relations experience. Full-time authors and travel writers, the two have such a large body of freelance work that when they reached more than 2,000 articles, stories and photographs published, they stopped counting. And the McKowens are well-respected ghostwriters, having worked with CEOs and founders of some of the nation's biggest companies. They have even ghostwritten for a former U.S. president and a few California governors and elected officials.

From 1999 to 2009, Ken and Dahlynn were consultants and coauthors for *Chicken Soup for the Soul*, where they collaborated with series founders Jack Canfield and Mark Victor Hansen on several books such as *Chicken Soup for the Entrepreneur's Soul; Chicken Soup for the Soul in Menopause; Chicken Soup for the Fisherman's Soul;* and *Chicken Soup for the Soul: Celebrating Brothers and Sisters*. They also edited and ghost-created many more Chicken titles during their tenure, with Dahlynn reading more than 100,000 story submissions.

For highly acclaimed outdoor publisher Wilderness Press, the McKowens' books include *Best of Oregon and Washington's Mansions, Museums and More; The Wine-Oh! Guide to California's Sierra Foothills* and national award-winning *Best of California's Missions, Mansions and Museums.*

Under the Publishing Syndicate banner, the couple authored and published *Wine Wherever: In California's Mid-Coast & Inland Region*, and are actively researching wineries for *Wine Wherever: In California's Paso Robles Region*, the second book in the Wine Wherever series.

Dahlynn with Tashi (1970)

NYMB Co-Creator

About Margie Yee Webb

Margie Yee Webb is the author and photographer of *Cat Mulan's Mindful Musings: Insight and Inspiration for a Wonderful Life.*

A resident of Northern California, Margie is involved with many writing groups. She has served as vice president of the California Writers Club (CWC). One of the nation's oldest professional clubs for writers, the CWC was founded by acclaimed author Jack London in 1909 (www.calwriters. org). Margie has also served many terms as president of the California Writers Club—Sacramento branch, where she received the Jack London Award for outstanding service in 2011.

Margie is a member of the Cat Writers' Association and the Women's National Book Association–San Francisco chapter. She is also one of several producers of the movie *FEMME: Women Healing the World.*

In regards to *Cat Mulan's Mindful Musings*, Margie was presented with certificates of excellence in the "gift" and "color photographs" series by the Cat Writers' Association for its 2011 Communications Contest. And in 2012, Margie was awarded "Best Nonfiction, Gift Category" and "Best

Book Design, 2nd Place" by the Northern California Publishers & Authors.

Margie supports several animal-welfare organizations and shelters in Northern California, including People for Animal Welfare in El Dorado County (PAWED), Happy Tails Pet Sanctuary and the Sacramento SPCA. She also donates to the San Francisco SPCA and ASPCA. If you are looking for a special pet to adopt, Margie recommends visiting www.petfinder.com.

Margie and Cat Mulan

Contributor Bios

Joan (JC) Andrew lives in Sedona, Arizona and is a professional artist and writer. She produces fiction, short stories and poetry. Her most recent project is the mystery *Painted Death*, a book based on her experiences in Alaska. Contact: Andrew_arts@esedona.net

Robley J. Barnes is a Missourian who has lived in Arizona, Alabama, Kentucky, Tennessee, Louisiana and now Plano, Texas. He is a retired industrial adhesive chemist and a prolific writer of rhymes. A 50-plus year marriage has produced two daughters and four grandchildren. Contact: rbarstar32@hotmail.com

Valerie D. Benko writes from Pennsylvania where she lives with her husband and an ever-rotating cast of rescued cats. She has written for other NYMB titles and has more than two dozen essays and short stories published in the U.S. and Canada. Visit her online at http://valeriebenko.weebly.com.

Jordan Bernal is the author of *The Keepers of Éire*, a dragon fantasy that encourages adult readers to let their imaginations take flight. Love of fantasy inspires her to write and publish through her company, Dragon Wing Publishing. She currently serves as president of Tri-Valley Writers. Follow Jordan at http://www.jordanbernal.com.

Debra Ayers Brown is a freelance writer, blogger, magazine columnist and award-winning marketing professional. Enjoy her stories in *Not Your Mother's Books*, *Chicken Soup for the Soul*, *Guideposts*, *Woman's World* and more. She graduated with honors from UGA and earned her MBA from The Citadel. Please visit www.DebraAyersBrown.com and www.About.Me/DebraAyersBrown.

Shannon Brown is the author of *Rock'N'Roll in Locker Seventeen*, a humorous young-adult novel. She also runs www.tshirtfort.com, a funny-gift website. Shannon lives in the San Francisco Bay Area. Her writer's website is www.locker17.com.

Dr. Stephanie Burk—aka "Doc Steph"—is a southwestern Ohio veterinarian who pursues reading, writing, traveling, gardening and all things equestrian in her not-so-copious spare time. She sounds off occasionally at www.dogphysicsandotherobservations.blogspot.com and hopes to write a blockbuster novel when she grows up.

Barbara Carpenter contributes to numerous anthologies and her stories appear in several NYMB titles. At work on her sixth book, she enjoys various activities. She and her husband reside beside a small lake in Illinois, where they love spending time with their two children, four grandchildren and two great-grandsons.

Michele Cemo lives in California with husband Ken and their two adult daughters. They rescue feral cats, have them spayed or neutered then release them. Any kittens they find are tamed and adopted out to loving homes. They have helped more than 45 cats thus far, and are still counting!

Carol Commons-Brosowske is a native Texan. She's been married 40 years to her husband, Jim. She has three grown children and is excitedly expecting her first grandchild. Carol has been published in *Not Your Mothers Books* and *Chicken Soup for the Soul* and writes a weekly column for *Frank Talk* magazine.

Harriet Cooper is a freelance writer and humorist. Her cat-related pieces have been featured in *Animal Wellness, I Luv Cats, Cup of Comfort, The Globe and Mail, The Montreal Gazette, Alive, Suite101, MeowBox* and *Chicken Soup*. She is currently working on an anthology of humorous cat stories. Contact: shewrites@live.ca

Susan Easterly is an award-winning writer and author of *Your Older Cat and The Guide to Handraising Kittens*. A professional member of the Cat Writers' Association (CWA), Susan is currently the poetry contributing editor of *laJoie*, a quarterly publication dedicated to promoting appreciation for all beings. Contact: poetsleapse@gmail.com

Terri Elders lives near Colville, Washington, with dog, Nat, and mismatched feline triplets. Akita Tsunami passed away recently, never having devoured a single cat. A lifelong writer and editor, Terri is a regular contributor to *Not Your Mother's Book*. She co-created *Not Your Mother's Book...On Travel*. She blogs at http://atouchoftarragon.blogspot.com.

Karin Frank is an award-winning author who lives on a farm in the Kansas City area. Her work has been published in a wide variety of venues, both in the U.S. and abroad. Her first book of poems, *A Meeting of Minds*, was released in April 2012.

T'Mara Goodsell, who lives near St. Louis, Missouri, has written for various anthologies, newspapers and publications. She is working on a book for young adults and was recently adopted by none other than "The Great Catsby."

Dianna Graveman is author of over 160 articles, co-author of four regional histories, and a co-creator of *NYMB...On Being a Mom*. She provides editorial and design services through 2 Rivers Communications & Design and in partnership with Treehouse Author Services. Find her at www.diannagraveman.com and www.2riverscommunications.com.

Susan Guerrero has written professionally for several decades. She has a journalism degree from the University of Arizona in Tucson and has written for newspapers for many years. She has also written more than 1,600 posts for her online blog titled "Writing Straight from the Heart."

Stacey Gustafson is a humor columnist and blogger. Her short stories have appeared in *Chicken Soup for the Soul, Not Your Mother's Book, Erma Bombeck Writers' Workshop, Midlife Boulevard* and *More Magazine*. Stacey lives in California with her husband and two teenagers. Visit her blog at www.staceygustafson.com or Twitter @ RUKiddingStacey.

Dena Harris is the author of several books including the popular *Does This Collar Make My Butt Look Big? A Diet Book For Cats* from Random House. Dena is a senior content creator for The Sales Factory + Woodbine marketing agency and lives in Greensboro, North Carolina with Snowball the Cat.

Julie Hatcher lives in South Carolina with her husband, two sons and two attention-seeking cats. She's been a full-time mom for the past 13 years. Unsure if a counseling degree has helped with raising kids, she's certain raising kids has helped her writing.

Stacey Hatton is co-author of the best-selling books *I Just Want to Pee Alone* and *I Just Want to Be Alone*. Humor columnist, member of the National Society of Newspaper Columnists and Erma Bombeck Writers' Workshops attendee, she's frequently on *KC Live!* TV. Email: nursemommylaughs@yahoo.com, Blog: http://NurseMommyLaughs.com

Cliff Johnson graduated from Cal Poly Pomona in 1972. He spent 30 years in prison—in uniform and administration—and was finally released (retired) in 1995. He and wife Scharre live in the most beautiful place on earth—Crescent City, California. And Cliff's daughter, Dahlynn, is now in possession of the killer piano.

Janet Sheppard Kelleher authored *Big C, little ta-tas*, an inspirational look at how she used humor to cope with—and kick—breast cancer's butt. A Southern columnist, Janet's love of finding humor in life sparked her mini-memoir, *Havin' My Cotton-Pickin' Say*. Both books are scheduled to debut in 2014. Contact: gop53her@gmail.com

Julaina Kleist-Corwin published an anthology in 2014 called *Written Across the Genres*. She is an award-winning writer and her short stories are published in the *California Writers Club Literary Review*, Harlequin's Christmas books and other anthologies. She teaches creative writing in Dublin and Pleasanton, California. Visit her at www.timetowritenow.com.

Nancy Julien Kopp writes creative nonfiction, memoir, inspirational, poetry, award-winning children's fiction and articles on the writing craft. She's published in 14 *Chicken Soup for the Soul* books, other anthologies, newspapers, ezines and Internet radio. She blogs about the writing world with tips for writers at www.writergrannysworld.blogspot.com.

Myron Kukla is a Midwest freelance writer living in Holland, Michigan, the tulip capital of the world. He is the author of several books of humor including *Guide to Surviving Life* and two e-books on Amazon. Contact: myronkukla@gmail.com

Lisa McManus Lange is published in many anthologies; this is her fifth *Not Your Mother's Book* story with Publishing Syndicate. An office worker, mother, writer and cat-keeper, Lisa lives in Victoria, BC, Canada where she also writes young-adult fiction. You can find her at www.lisamcmanuslange.blogspot.com or email her at lisamc2010@yahoo.ca.

Mary Laufer is a substitute teacher in Central Florida. Her essays, short stories and poems have been published in 35 anthologies, including *NYMB...On Being a Mom, NYMB...On Being a Parent, A Shaker of Margaritas* and in several volumes of *Chicken Soup for the Soul* and *A Cup of Comfort*.

Rieva Lester is a journalist who lives in Winlock, Washington. In addition to being Super-Mom, she's highly skilled at setting up camp, playing cribbage, winning at poker, rescuing cats from walls and paying too much for car insurance.

Steve Liddick is the author of three novels, a memoir of his 47 years in the radio business and a camping cookbook. He and his wife, Sherry, live near Sacramento, California with their horse, three donkeys and five cats.

Glady Martin lives in a small hamlet in British Columbia, Canada, where she enjoys sharing her stories through words. Having written since grade school, she says, "Writing is a way of breathing for me . . . it is a wonderful tool for expressing myself." Email: gladymartin1@shaw.ca

Mary McGrath is a freelance writer and photographer based in Culver City, California. Her work has appeared in several publications including *Newsweek, Westways Magazine, Good Housekeeping, LA Times, The National Lampoon* and many other publications. For more information: www.marymcgrathphotography.com.

Mike McHugh is author of "The Dang Yankee," a humorous column about life in Louisiana and the world at large. His column appears in *Jambalaya News*, a publication covering Southwest Louisiana and Southeast Texas. This is his third contribution to the NYMB series.

Angela McKeown is a humor writer whose blog—Momopolize.com—was voted Circle of Moms' Top 25 Family Blogs. Angela's four boisterous boys provide plenty of funny writing material. Warning: Don't ask her about her kids or she will Momopolize the conversation! Contact: momopolize@gmail.com

Sheila Moss is a weekly humor columnist and has been published by Voyager Press, McGraw Hill and Oxford Press. Her stories appear in *Guidepost's* anthologies, as well as in numerous other publications. She is past web editor for National Society of Newspaper Columnists, founder of the Southern Humorists group and publisher of HumorColumnist.com.

Pat Nelson, writer, editor and workshop presenter on anthologies and on finding your story, is co-creator of *NYMB...On Being a Parent* and the upcoming *NYMB...On Working for a Living*. Her stories appear in *The Valley Bugler* and at www.LewisRiver.com. Visit her at www.Storystorm.US.

Sheree K. Nielsen, author of *Folly Beach Dances*—a healing coffee-table book—is an award-winning writer, photographer and poet. Publications include *Missouri Life, AAA Midwest, Southern Traveler, Carolina Go!* and countless anthologies, newspapers and websites. Follow Sheree at www.shereenielsen.wordpress.com, @ShereeKNielsen and @follybeachdance on Twitter. Official book website: www.beachdances.com

Risa Nye lives in Oakland, California. She co-edited *Writin' on Empty* (available on Amazon and Kindle). Her articles and essays have appeared in local and national publications and in several anthologies. She writes about the craft of nonfiction for *Hippocampus Magazine (*HippocampusMagazine.com*)*. Her "Ms. Barstool" cocktail column appears online at Berkeleyside.com.

Susan Whitley Peters lives in Mission, Kansas, and teaches writing and grammar at a local community college. She is on the board of The Writers Place in Kansas City, and her poetry and prose has appeared in numerous online and print publications. Contact: swpetersksusa@yahoo.com

Marsha Porter has written thousands of movie reviews, hundreds of articles, dozens of short stories and a monthly column. She broke into writing when the 500-word essay was the punishment du jour at her Catholic school.

Janda Rangel, wife and mother of three married children, enjoys writing about the funny side of life. Her grandkids—Ethan and Elliot—keep her laughing and grounded. After teaching for 28 years, she decided to put her training to work and is currently crafting several short stories for publication. Jandarangel@gmail.com

Cappy Hall Rearick is a syndicated newspaper columnist, award-winning short-story writer and author of six published books and five successful columns. Featured by the Erma Bombeck Writers' Workshop as a Humor Writer of the Month, Rearick's humor and short fiction have been read and enjoyed in anthologies throughout the country.

John Reas, a financial services consultant in the Dallas area, has two amazing daughters in college and a wonderful wife. The cats in John's life have all been replaced by dogs, of which three are currently living in the Reas home. This is his fifth story in the NYMB series.

Roger Riley grew up in America's heartland. Country living and enjoyment of the simple pleasures of life in a time before television, radio and technology were readily available in his small town, made him an avid fan of all genres. Writing has always been both entertainment and a creative outlet for him.

Sioux Roslawski is catless right now, but she has a whole herd of Golden Retrievers and rescues dogs for the organization "Love a Golden." She's a third-grade teacher by day and a freelance writer on the weekends. More of Sioux's writing can be found at http://siouxspage.blogspot.com.

Julie Royce, an attorney, published *PILZ*, a crime thriller, and is writing a sequel. She is also currently working on a fictionalized biography, *Ardent Spirit,* about Odawa-French fur trader Magdelaine Laframboise. Julie has published two travel books, written magazine articles and is included in several anthologies. Check her out at www.jkroyce.com.

John Evangelist Schlimm II is the international award-winning author of *Stand Up!: 75 Young Activists Who Rock the World, And How You Can, Too!, The Ultimate Beer Lover's Happy Hour* and a 2015 memoir about Sr. Augustine. Also an activist, artist and educator, he holds a master's from Harvard University. www.JohnSchlimm.com

Joyce Newman Scott worked as a flight attendant while pursuing an acting career. She started college in her 50s and studied at the University of Miami and at Florida International University. She has contributed short stories to *Chicken Soup for the Soul* and *Not Your Mother's Book*. Contact Joyce at jnewmansco@aol.com.

Janice Singer developed a love of writing short stories upon attending a writing workshop in January of 2011. She is a transplanted Iowa girl living in Florida with her husband and their current cat, Ally. Janice writes about growing up in the Midwest and the crazy adventures of her cats.

Rosie Sorenson, award-winning author of *They Had Me at Meow*, is a humor columnist at www.foolishtimes.net and frequent contributor to www.humorwriters.org and other publications. Her memoir, *Stray Love: How Turtleman and the Homeless Cats of Buster Hollow Fixed My Broken Heart*, is due out in 2015. Email: RosieSorenson29@yahoo.com

Cheryl Anne Stapp lives in Sacramento, California, with her husband Murry. A retired accountant-turned-historian, she is the author of the award-winning *Disaster & Triumph: Sacramento Women, Gold Rush Through the Civil War* and two other books published by the History Press. Follow her blog "California's Olden Golden Days" at http://cherylannestapp.com.

Barbara Stretton is the author of three YA novels and a mystery series about a cat detective named Tori Trotter. She is also an award-winning painter of oils, acrylics and pastels. Her favorite subject is cats—she and her husband currently have seven lively ones. To learn more, visit www.ToriTrotter.com.

Janine V. Talbot and her husband Chuck reside in southern Maine where they raised their two daughters. She has been published online and writes a weekly humor column for a local newspaper. Her humorous blog on marriage, motherhood, menopause and the newly-empty nest is at www.momofmanywords.com. Contact: momofmanywords@gmail.com

Roselie Thoman is a mother, writer and educator. She lives in the Pacific Northwest with her husband, two children, a yellow Lab and a mischievous cat. When not chasing wildlife out of the house or children around the house, she finds time to write.

Lisa Tognola, a freelance writer who pens the blog Mainstreetmusingsblog. com, highlights the humorous side of suburban life—the good, the bad and the ugly. She is a columnist at *The Alternative Press* and contributes to online magazine More.com. Twitter @lisatognola

Tina Wagner-Mattern is a Portland, Oregon, writer who is married to a great guy, has two awesome kids and a spoiled-rotten cat named Sauza. She is grateful to have been published in eight other mainstream anthologies. Contact her at tinamattern@earthlink.net.

Pat Wahler is a grant writer by day and writer of fiction and essays by night. Her work can be found in both national and local publications. A lifelong animal lover, Pat ponders critters, writing and life's little mysteries at www.critteralley.blogspot.com.

Ernie Witham writes the nationally-syndicated column, "Ernie's World," for the *Montecito Journal* in Santa Barbara, California. He is also the author of two humor books and leads humor-writing workshops in several cities. He is on the permanent faculty of the Santa Barbara Writers Conference.

Pamela Wright is a freelance humor writer from Atlanta, Georgia. She lives with two cats named Zelda and Gracie, affectionately known as "The Old Maid Starter Kit." Pamela's writing has previously been published on *Full Grown People* and in the *Atlanta Journal-Constitution*.

Story Permissions

Photo Credits

Except as indicated below, the photos in this book were provided by the story contributors and used with their permission.

Cover photo: Sarah Fields Photography/Shutterstock.com
Page 46: Kathleene Baker, *On Duty*
Page 106: Ethan Allison, *Eddie the Car Cat*
Page 124: Paula Chinick, *The Pen Gremlin*
Page 188: Mary Ann Sit, *Talk to the Paw*

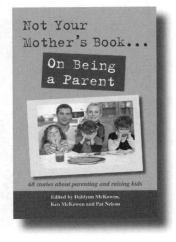